THE THRONE OF THE
THIRD HEAVEN OF THE
NATIONS MILLENNIUM
GENERAL ASSEMBLY

Also by Denis Johnson

The Man Among the Seals
Inner Weather
The Incognito Lounge
The Veil
Angels
Fiskadoro
The Stars at Noon
Resuscitation of a Hanged Man
Jesus' Son

THE THRONE OF THE THIRD HEAVEN OF THE NATIONS MILLENNIUM GENERAL ASSEMBLY

POEMS COLLECTED
=== AND NEW ===

DENIS JOHNSON

HarperCollins*Publishers*

The Man Among the Seals was originally published by Stone Wall Press, *Inner Weather* by Graywolf Press, *The Incognito Lounge* by Random House and reprinted by Carnegie Mellon Press, and *The Veil* by Alfred A. Knopf. "Our Sadness" appeared in *Tendril* magazine; "Iowa City," "Grocery on Venice Beach," "On the Morning of a Wedding," and "Orchard" appeared in *Trafika*; and "Visits," "Drink," and "A Saint" appeared in *South Ash Review*.

HarperCollins books may be purchased for educational, business, or sales promotional use. For information, please e-mail the Special Markets Department at SPsales@harpercollins.com.

FIRST EDITION

Designed by Gloria Adelson/LuLu Graphics

Library of Congress Cataloging-in-Publication Data

Johnson, Denis, 1949–
    The throne of the third heaven of the nations millennium general assembly : poems, collected and new / Denis Johnson.
        p.   cm.
    ISBN 978-0-06-092696-0
    I. Title.
    PS3560.03745T48   1995
    811'.54—dc20   95-3170

HB 11.08.2017

The Throne of the Third Heaven of the Nations Millennium General Assembly was constructed by James Hampton (1909–1964), a janitor for the General Services Administration, over a fourteen-year period from 1950 until the time of his death, after which it was discovered in a garage he rented near his apartment in Washington, D.C. Made of scavenged materials, minutely detailed and finished with glittering foil, The Throne occupies an area of some two hundred square feet and stands three yards in height at its center. It has a room to itself in the National Museum of American Art in Washington, D.C.

CONTENTS

The Man Among the Seals

Inner Weather

The Incognito Lounge

The Veil

New Poems

THE MAN AMONG THE SEALS

"Did you have rapport with the seals?" the judge asked.

"I guess I did have rapport with the seals," Giordano said.

Despite the rapport, Basel fined Giordano $50 for annoying the seals.

—AP *Wire Service*

Quickly Aging Here

I

nothing to drink in
the refrigerator but juice from
the pickles come back
long dead, or thin
catsup. i feel i am old

now, though surely i
am young enough? i feel that i have had
winters, too many heaped cold

and dry as reptiles into my slack skin.
i am not the kind to win
and win.
no i am not that kind, i can hear

my wife yelling, "goddamnit, quit
running over," talking to
the stove, yelling, "i
mean it, just stop," and i am old and

2

i wonder about everything: birds
clamber south, your car
kaputs in a blazing, dusty
nowhere, things *happen*, and constantly you

wish for your slight home, for

your wife's rusted
voice slamming around the kitchen. so few

of us wonder why
we crowded, as strange,
monstrous bodies, blindly into one
another till the bed

choked, and our range
of impossible maneuvers was gone,
but isn't it because by dissolving like so
much dust into the sheets we are crowding

south, into the kitchen, into
nowhere?

Boy Aged Six Remembering

this has been a
busy day. in the morning there was
his mother, calling to him
from the garden and he ran
thinking that he was

a tower into the light around her.
he had wanted to
bring her water, or a
small thing. later

he will perhaps harness the afternoon
and send it ahead to pull
us down, or up, who can
say for later?

now is the thing, now
with the light around the house
in the yard and earlier,
before lunch, when he saw his father

at the well sending the pail
far down into the cooler, hidden
water; earlier, when he saw
his father reaching down like

that into the water, and did not
recognize the composition of a
memory, or how they, these people, are
often composed of memories.

Victory

the woman whose face has just finished breaking
with a joy so infinite

and heavy that it might be grief has won
a car on a giveaway show, for her family,

for an expanse of souls that washes from a million
picture tubes onto the blank reaches

of the air. meanwhile, the screams are packing
the air to a hardness: in the studio

the audience will no longer move, will be caught
slowly, like ancient, staring mammals, figuring

out the double-cross within the terrible progress
of a glacier. here, i am suddenly towering

with loneliness, repeating to this woman's
only face, *this time, again, i have not won.*

Spring

by now even the ground
deep under the ground has dried.
the grass becoming green

does not quite remember the last year,
or the year before, or the centuries
that kept passing over. all of these blades thought
that america's grief over the ruptured

flesh of its leaders
was another wind going into the sky.
a rabbit stiffens

with hard sorrow up from the grass
and runs. well,
it is another spring and in the clouds

it is the ranging spectacle of a crowd
of congressmen accusing one another, each
moving in his own shadow against the next.

Why I Might Go to the Next Football Game

sometimes you know
things: once at a
birthday party a little

girl looked at her new party
gloves and said she
liked me, making suddenly the light much
brighter so that the very small

hairs shone above her lip. i felt
stuffed, like a swimming pool, with
words, like i knew something that was in
a great tangled knot. and when we sat

down i saw there were
tiny glistenings on her
legs, too. i knew
something for sure then. but it

was too big, or like the outside too
everywhere, or maybe
hiding inside, behind
the bicycles where i later

kissed her, not using my tongue. it was
too giant and thin to squirm
into, and be so well inside of, or
too well hidden to punch, and feel. a few

days later on the asphalt playground i
tackled her. she skinned her

elbow, and i even
punched her and felt her, felt

how soft the hairs were. i thought
that i would make a fine football-playing
poet, but now i know
it is better to be an old, breathing

man wrapped in a great coat in the stands, who
remains standing after each play, who knows
something, who rotates in his place
rasping over and over the thing

he knows: "whydidnhe *pass*? the other
end was wide *open*! the end
was wide *open*! the end was wide *open* . . ."

A Woman Is Walking Alone Late at Night

no one can know through what silence she moves. for long
nights, through an eternity of stealth
she has tracked her own dim form drifting there
ahead, has seen her
self, lost again, keep swimming through this wealth
of solitude. it must be wrong,

that i should watch her. i'm afraid that she
will turn her eyes to me, show me the fast
outdistancing of years she sees, and i
would clutch terribly
after my past days as if for the last
thing i would see, as if for me
all those long moments, each friendly second i'd known
was lost, gone to the air, was really gone.

The Dry Dry Land. Here

the dry dry land. here
and there from the
rasp and muscle of its flatness
a tree gushes forth. i

have seen trees, have
heard them at night being
dragged into the sky.
i know that they are very
real. i know they know.

lover, i am not
a tree, you would
never mistake me
for one, my arid movements

for its flowing coolness. but
sometimes in the dark silken
air of this room

i feel that we are
a liquid jumble of trees
falling interminably away from
the land, its dry infinitude.

The Glimpsed Old Woman in the Supermarket

from the sidewalk i can see her,
as she barely stands, easily mired
among supermarket products,
as if rapidly and all
too soon the swimming hole
had turned solid. around her,

housewives search for a detergent
that will cleanse away the years;
locking her vision into
a box of tide she must see
the finances crumbling
in the distant bank, or the remembered
friends, who she knew
would be winding up here.

i cannot touch
you. i would like to hold you forth
and say, here is the television
sign-off music; this
is the vision crept up on
by cloudiness, first in the corners;
here is the morning

trickling from the house. but i can't
reach you: just as easily the sidewalk
holds me, and i love you,
i want to crook my finger beneath
your dress, and unearth
your trembling, delicate loins.

Poem Questioning the Existence of the Sea

in exactly the same
way that the animals were launched
onto the sand, frightened

after so many eons by the sudden
darkness of the sea,
a very large number

of children plunge daily in their last great
evolutionary spasm from the wombs
of pale, inarticulate women. it is wide

and kind of empty where one stands,
now, years after, and floats
drastically his hips

against the pin-ball machine. outside,
the detective wail of his own
impossible child is overturning the streets,

as he maneuvers this unloveable machine, deftly
and like a great ship,
through the stages of his life. just

as confused as ever, i observe
the buildings increasing under the sky,
knowing that soon i must

become him, and elude
my children and bludgeon the waves
in skillful drunkenness. i tremble,

like an old indian, for just a little
rain over this desert.

Telling the Hour

if you want to know
the time you must look
at a clock, or stare continuously
into the moon,

until it grows round like a clock.
under the moon growing round
a hunter strolls; he must be saying,

"i have killed an animal." however,
as the evening draws
close in for a better look, it is

nine p.m. and the hunter's arms
are loaded with air, his belly
swells with the solitude. he is saying,
"i *think* i have killed an animal,

a barely visible bird,
at eight p.m., or the dim
figure of a woman bent over
her sewing, in a distant house,

who glanced occasionally
at the big moon. and i shot
a telephone pole as it strained
into the sky, wanting desperately the moon."

as he continues among the trees,
the ticking of the city becomes
larger, moving the birds and insects

from the air, rattling

the moon so that it opens
and tolls down upon the hunter.
his hands try to caress the sudden,
awkward hush, and he wonders more often,
"have i killed an animal?"

Retirement

i would like to be just an old man with my gin,
retiring even from these leaves into
my big, gradual silence beyond the wood
and it will be good,
wife, because i have pointed to you,
and you have become real. within

this darker stillness my eyes grow too wide.
it must be that seeing you in the trees
becoming softer than i ever dreamed
has made it all seem
a multitude of nonsense, all the seas,
the planets, all i wrote. i lied,

i swear to you i lied, becoming old and so
very drunk, when i did not lie to you.

The Year's First Snow

emptying into
the freezing, quiet alleys

there is the voice of a single
ferreting drunk. if he is singing

it is lovely, and if he talks on
strangely, he, at least,

understands. by the river, noiselessly,
some lovers have frozen

in the winter, and they will be taken
away, with the floods of spring.

in an upper window
of the county jail, the sleepless man

who was framed knows
that all along, all along,

this snow that rests
more heavily over the reach of branches

has been descending.

On a Busy Street a Man Walks Behind a Woman

there is the chance that you will step
ahead of me into the traffic
alive, and that there will be
an accident. always i am walking,

i am seeing your heels and thinking
of something else, but always i am
asking you to remember: if you step carefully

into the screeching
of tires and become bloody, i must not
be the one extending himself awkwardly

into the confusion to say, my dear
mrs. hutchins, do
forgive the way we have arranged

your body, dead like that
on the pavement, but surely you
understand? it must
not be me who is the one

fisherman to fish you up drowned among
all that seaweed. it cannot
be me looking in all
directions for help, knowing all

along that it is just you
and me, finally, and that i am
alone to hear the sound of the breakfast
bell opening as it did

into the corners of the barnyard, and your
mother's voice calling back
and forth among the animals. am i

positioned here alone to welcome
you from such a very distant
place, and must i now tell you what every

second in your life, what all the
breathing and the continual inching
forward of the body through each and every
day, when i am so absolutely

young, when i am so
unprepared, must i
tell you what it has all
at last come to? you are

dead, mrs. hutchins, amid this
mob craning to see your own blood,
which has somehow

gotten away from you in all
the excitement—i am so truly sorry,
of course it isn't fair, you weren't
prepared, but don't you see it works

this way for all of us, for instance that
i am here just isn't fair, either, because
of my unpreparedness, because of my lack

of anything to say except you're dead,
you're dead, i didn't
do it, i didn't do it.

Checking the Traps

morning,
the door opening, changing
into a doorway. half

the night i stayed awake and smoked
and watched the mousetraps.
the mice were there, nudging
into cups and plates, one fell

into the toaster, but escaped.
they waited until i gave up and slept to die.
for these mice
the night will be long. i heard

the iron snapping
in my sleep and dreamed my wife was
closing the door.

two mice are dead, for my wife.
mice make her legs
go watery, as they do sometimes after her climax.

one mouse's head is barely
in the trap, one eye probing
toward the ceiling where i could tell him
there is nothing.
the other mouse is flung willingly under the iron

bar. i wonder, were they
married? was she pregnant? they are
going out together,

in the garbage this morning. it was
morning when we were married.
it has been morning

for a long time. that mouse, with his
eye. did he hear the iron snapping,
and dream it was his

wife with her stretching, laden tits
closing the door?

The Man Among the Seals

for Ed Schroeder

at night here in the park it is different:

the man by the seal pool stalks
through an acute emptiness, encircled
by the city. is he
taking off his clothes?

by day i have seen
the seals, enclosed, blundering
among the spattered rocks. they climb
like prisoners of a ferris wheel, above
their pool and above
the peanuts floating through
air, high over the sudden, too large

teeth of the spectators. but at night
without their land-locked captors moving
gracefully by, the seals
seem less inept, even

on the hostile rocks.
before dawn they rise
and dive, becoming masters
in the water. the figure in

underwear on the left is not
a seal. before me and
an audience of trees he has
joined the seals. drunk, perhaps,

and, a staggerer on land,
perhaps he hopes to move cleanly,
like a seal, through water. or,

sober, perhaps he dives to assume
the clumsiness now shed by the seals: then
he will tumble drunk onto
the ground, and the seals, plunging

landward, will find
no awkwardness among the rocks, will
no longer wonder deep
within themselves at a dry hardness
which is not ice. each day

he will return, wetness
forever staining through his pants,
to watch his seals as they rise
above the rocks to pluck the floating

bits of food, as they slide through
the air over the trees, the
ferris wheel grown

stationary with shame, the tiny
unfamiliar bodies jerking
under balloons through the lighted park.

Crossing Over the Ice

i should have brought
an axe to this white place and seen
for sure if, far beneath,
a city is falling irretrievably away.
as it is i can only guess

that this spot, warmer
than the rest, is where the tallest
steeple was cut loose to unmoor the town.
i wonder: could i nudge my vision

over onto the spaces below?
it has thus far been
easy to locate myself, somewhere between hands
warming in pockets and the hands that waken,
empty, out of the shadows
of buildings. i know

what's going on; the stars
evade the oceans, thank goodness,
and just here there are
the trees fumbling with roots under the earth.
to chip through to a town

that will not come back might
put me anywhere, i might become
that someone on the farther bank, who is standing

still within the movement of trees, as if
one step would lose him gradually
into the stars. he may be

THE MAN AMONG THE SEALS   25

the one who has leaned
his head into the air underneath and seen
another dawn glowing like a deep fish,
seen, as here above,

the citizens in the morning
growing tinier, weightless
and lost from their families,
preparing for beautiful
supermarkets, for an endlessness
of downward flight under an expanse of snow.

Upon Waking

at the far edge of earth, night
is going away. another
poem begins. slumped over

the typewriter i must get this
exactly, i want to make it
clear this morning that your

face, as it opens
from its shadow, is more
perfect than yesterday; and

that the light, as it
hesitates over the approach
of your smile, has given this

aching bed more than warmth,
more than poems; someway

a generous rose, or a very
delicate arrangement of sounds,
has come to peace in this new room.

A Child Is Born in the Midwest

as i look on your struggle i remember
i have seen arriving from movie theaters
the forms of people
disgraced, slanting heavily out of the cold,
their coats, the muscles under the skin
fraying, given up to the air.
and later, near morning,
i have seen their figures compelled
from the panic and emptiness of the town asleep
into all-night diners, which flounder, exhausted.
outside the towns the wide plains
are delirious
with frozen animals,
and the sky is rising with moons and moons.
these faces lifted over the street

are not moons. even so, they are
lost somewhere between worlds and home,
in a town that can't quite hold onto the earth.
i listen to your tiny,
unbelieving anguish,
and i wonder if i have known
these faces in another time;
and i think that you have come here, drifting
through universes of cold
because no longer, no longer
could the womb contain your loneliness.

To Enter Again

for the astronauts on the occasion
of their re-entry

for the first few instants in
this jungled machine we were all
at once human. then
we became confused monsters,
and then we were, as before,

sardines waiting to land hung
over like sardines.
for the first few instants
we had been dragged
outside of everything. but

the cracks began to show, each
of us was too much the
other, and we were once

again inside our terribly good
balloon, revolving and knowing
far too much.

the first day we slept
little, we examined and counted
the stars. we thought we should. and now
we sleep most of the time, dreaming

ourselves away from this haze
of tubes and gauges. we have learned: we
have been brought here to

wait, and to learn

to live packed
in forever, waiting to be pried
out. to live here truly
washed by the sea, turning end
over end, waiting to halt,

and breathe, but never
halting. waiting to slide at
last toward the freshly lighted

earth, there to wait and dive again far
down into tubes and fantasies.
the moon lies
there beyond us, cringing toward the neat

package of stars, not
waiting. below, in dreams, the earth scatters
in all directions way from
itself, and yearns
toward us, toward our distant perfection.

Drunk in the Depot

for Bob Zimmerman

drunk here in the railway depot
i can recall your train budging
forward in that other depot, that first
squash of steam making
your window real and solid. that is

why i am jumping down onto
the tracks, or because i am a gazelle.
i left later, by bus, and now
the city is gray and vacant, so i

am bounding out of the depot along
the tracks though i think
i am here to see someone
off. the train moved and you were

windowed in and everything was
final. or i might have left
by plane from the airport. no,

it was bus. i am supposed to
wave goodbye to a girl. that
was the last time i

saw you, so i will keep
moving down the tracks because
i *am* some kind of zebra, because
these railway tracks are mashing
like ridiculous snowshoes into

the distance. she thinks i am

cute, in a grubby, nonsexual
way. it was summer then; now
it is winter, with all
the roads stationed outside

the houses and the snow coming
to get them. it should have been
night, and it is.

The Cabinet Member

. . . wake up in the morning:
a critical editorial, or a Herb Block cartoon.
                    RICHARD NIXON

wake up
in the morning: a critical
editorial, or a herb block
cartoon. sometimes, if my wife

would just leave me alone things
would be all right. you should see
this cartoon,
or the poor sogginess
of this bacon, you don't believe this

country's going down
and not up. the sewers
demand attention. the potomac

is swallowing up all the love,
and society is
killing itself, for love. if i

had a dog there would be
more love in it for me. if
i had something in my hands.

In a Rented Room

this is a good dream, even if the falling is
no less real, and even if my feet will crumble

on the lurking ground. my throat itches, and i am
awake in this room which is no less vacant for

all my presence and there are no aspirin. here
is the sun with its tired surprise, the morning. there

are the cars and streets moving in the usual
fashion. the room wants to be rid of me. it must

fall open and communicate with other dim,
stifled rooms when i have slaughtered my body in

the sheets and fumbled streetward to sooth the itch. what
do you learn, room? what have you told, why are the stains

and the accusing glasses pointing so when i
return? there was the girl some time ago. *she* would

want to know where the guilt comes from, that hums over
the bed and descends, like an uncaring thumb, to

blot me out. she would help me, when the universe
has fooled me again, and the joke has gone too far,

when the itch, climbing, deep, remains after bottle
after bottle, and i inch toward death and i

must poke my body into a thousand vacant
darknesses before i strike the correct sleep, and dream.

Driving Toward Winter

miraculously,
there is the sun, coming back.
beneath it the cows wander, more
exhausted, baffled by the sparseness
of the winter grass. were i
a cow staggering over vanishing grass,

i would feel like the man
in the story, the one where
he leaps into his sports car to find
that everything has become an ocean, saying
certainly i did not expect
the sea. yesterday the numerous
actual cars spilled over
solid hills. kissing

my wife i never wished for the sea. in
an agony of exactness, bent
into the tiny measuring dials i did not
yearn for these impossible waves,
or for the stopped movement
of trees. the wrecked,
liquid countryside unfolds
beyond me, and i am the last bubble of air,
searching for air.

licking bare dirt, the nearest cow
raises his head to me, not understanding.
i would tell him about the sun, how it
rolls nearer, hauling the spring.

but he peers at me as if through mist, as i
would peer through the fogged, cracking windows
of my fast car at the half-
distinguished movements of an unusual fish.

A Poem about Baseballs

for years the scenes bustled
through him as he dreamed he was
alive. then he felt real, and slammed

awake in the wet sheets screaming
too fast, everything moves
too fast, and the edges of things
are gone. four blocks away

a baseball was a dot against
the sky, and he thought, my
glove is too big, i will

drop the ball and it will be
a home run. *the snow falls*
too fast from the clouds,
and night is dropped and

snatched back like a huge
joke. is that the ball, or is
it just a bird, and the ball is
somewhere else, and i will
miss it? *and the edges are gone, my*

hands melt into the walls, my
hands do not end where the wall
begins. should i move
forward, or back, or will the ball

come right to me? i know i will
miss, because i always miss when it

takes so long. *the wall has no*
surface, no edge, the wall

fades into the air and the air is
my hand, and i am the wall. my
arm is the syringe and thus i

become the nurse, i am you,
nurse. if he gets
around the bases before the
ball comes down, is it a home

run, even if i catch it? *if we could*
slow down, and stop, we
would be one fused mass careening
at too great a speed through
the emptiness. if i catch

the ball, our side will
be up, and i will have to bat,
and i might strike out.

The Woman at the Slot Machine

if the children were not locked
into georgia, and texas, if

the husband were not packed away
cold, never to be fished

from air, the plunging down
of the handle might be less desperate

but alone now before
this last enemy, she juggles

for any victory. the jerked
handle offers a possible coming home. each

symbol come to rest clicks into
her eyes, because

it *is* there to be had, it
was there once, the old miracle come back

alive, when the bell
sang like a beautiful daughter and it was

harry, upstairs with his broken
leg, ringing for her, yelling, martha come hear

the radio, it's jack benny and he's playing
the violin.

The Mourning in the Hallway

my neighbor's voice occurs within the hall, sadly:
come back inside the house awhile before
you go away. his daughter does not hear
his oldest voice swear
that he will balance forward from that door
forever toward the spaces she

has left. and even i have felt this thing,
this leaning into the ocean like wild,
like aching beasts. my wife was not alone
when, deep in her bone
and tumbling eternally, our child
continued drowning. now, hearing

this man's face change against the tide his girl has gone
away with, i leap to hold my own son.

Out There Where the Morning

out there where the morning
is, the automobiles and citizens
are clattering along just
like pieces of the universe. from

my place by the window i can
examine an airplane as it crawls
from speck to speck on the glass.
i know that it is with
the same arrogant mechanical

lust that the pipes of the kitchen sink
are dissolving. i am
ready to believe that everything else is,
too. for instance this
room i am sure is
atom by atom taking leave. but here in

the disappearing room i am not too
heavily alone. printed on the
label of this cookie can is
the one assurance:

each cookie contains a joke.

and i know that this
is somehow good. i can
call my mother and say, mother
it is not what is true, but what

is good that now matters. mother,
mother, even here in this tumbling
jar of selves,
each cookie contains a joke,

each of us offers himself up whole
to some nearly invisible,
tasteless affirmation.
such sensation as we derive is derived

only from the joke. mother,
i am this morning electric. i am spinning
into the staccato punch line,
the end and the crumbling. i will

hear the laughter as it breaks up
and dissolves farther out in space,
as it grinds and echoes against the metal.

In Praise of Distances

as the winter slips up under
the palms of my hands, it is getting
harder to be a poet: i am woe
itself. my car fades

without pain from the parking lot. it
crumples to one knee, like
an elephant, startled
into lifelessness by the hungry bullets of winter.
the graveyard wavers
distantly. the car will no longer stand

between me and the debts nuzzling
at my door. i will no longer go rattling
among the miles as if

distance were a safe thing, as if i slammed
the ancient car door
in the face of all the noises.
my wife tells me, why don't you get
a job? but once i had a dog,

whose vital organs became
confused beneath his skin, until he died;
i will not leave this animal kingdom

until he comes back from the trees.
i will keep my nostrils
opened for the lonely jangle
of his collar landing over the buildings

or for some sign that he will be returning.
my hands will not
be filled with advertisements; so

they will be filled with the difficulty
that is winter. if he is lost,
farmers hoping for spring will discover
his voice among the corn stalks,

seeking a safe place to lie
quietly down. as i wait for him
by the window,
i have the suspicion that the meaning of things
will never be sorted out.

A Consequence of Gravity

my wife's voice yelling from
the window holds the distant echoes
of a thousand mothers-in-law, all the women,
all the weight, increasing, of this planet.

i will not listen. here in the yard i am watching
an old story: a child has dived
into the earth attempting to fly, and injured

farther than the skin he gives
his long syllable toward the moon.
there is no one to tell him he will settle

for years, in a gradual re-enactment
of this flight, against the earth,
as he cries over his miserable attachment
to the ground and mourns

that first unlucky generation
of airplanes, the lost inventions still burrowing
somewhere desperately away from the air,
making caves, making

no sense at all crushed into the sides of mountains.
i grow, like an imprisoned pilot,
heavier, near death, my face
makes mistakes in the last oxygen of the cockpit.

through the dusk the moon has rolled
again out into her private ocean. i cannot
help it, like a blank virgin she has retired

beyond the air, and here, bereft, surrounded
by grotesque, inedible women and the painful
breaking of another spring i admit it,
i will never touch her, hold her.

For the Death of the Old Woman

one after another along
the perspective of the street, the people
remain upright. my hands

are blacking out, from the cold,
dry body of this old woman.
she has died,

while she was sitting, concerned
somewhere in her house. growing
more beautiful, something has left

the big rocker, has moved
through the leaves brushing her window,
beyond the trees and first

national bank to a point
overlooking the collapse of cities.
the rivers are backing up

with whales
and wreckage, with
the crowds of foam becoming huge and

hanging to the factories that lean
over the wettening banks.
the figures

of graves diminish toward
the horizon:
on the street,

these faces are not chipped with grief,
as they leap after busses.
in the window of a store front a man

who did not know her adjusts
the limbs of a mannequin, and
the ascending voice

of a child wants to know, do the rivers freeze
by themselves, can you walk on them.

The Man Who Was Killed

whatever the wind says that divides
the surface of the river

into tiny, upward gestures of surprise
is not known, not here

by me on the bank. i have wondered
this same thing about the wintry faces of pedestrians,

i have wondered how much of this
is crazy and how much is real. he must have been

hearing the wind, to be so deeply
startled when the bullet rushed

from the assassin's control. he remembers always
how it was, to breathe. his eye

drifts through the streets in the city,
through the rain, dreaming after his life.

April 20, 1969

when i think that i am watching
the evening lengthen toward the end of this country,
i know there can be no sea
at the end of the pier. even
the sea has gone to hide deep
in the spaces below the sea, and the few
children who have stayed this long in the yard
are disappearing toward their dinners.

INNER
WEATHER

An Evening with the Evening

The night is very tall
coming down the street. The light
of the streetlights coming on
in sequence just in front of the dark,
this light is a prison
broken loose from itself.
The city has an expression
on its face like that of someone hoping

he will not be noticed,
it is like that of the man now watching
the processional flaring of the lamps from the corner,
beneath the bank sign.
He notices the city, he notices
the reflection of his own face in the city,
he wonders what the city must have done

to the night,
that it should avert itself like a debtor
while welcoming the night
with such display, such grim pomp, so courteous
a removal, before
the arrival of darkness,
of any competing darknesses that may have
managed to precede it there.

Suddenly it is the total blackness
with the numerous small lights of the face
of the city shining through it;
then it is the end,

which is only himself, going
home to his wife and children,
turning and trying to walk away from the darkness
that precedes him, darkness of which he is the center.

Winter

On the streets, which have gutters,
in the shadows of doorways, at
busstops, at this moment
and yesterday, before the bars, their breath
excluded in great
clouds, turning from the wind
to spit
and laugh horribly

at the life standing up inside them
with such pain as
loneliness permits, and the weather,
turning to each other
with jokes and lies, with the baggage
and garbage of their humanness as if one
they held it toward would
take it and thank them

is us, all of us, all dragged by the legs upstream
like poor stooges sunk to drowning
for a living.
On Clinton St. the bars explode
with the salt smell of us like the sea, and the tide
of rock and roll music, live
humans floating on it
out over the crimes of the night. How

unlike such outwardness the clenching back
of a man into himself is,
several of us are our own fists
There! emphasizing on the tabletop.

Prayer: That We May Be Given This Day the Usual Business

Some days the automobiles are smiling,
other days they
are morose;
and so it is with humans, always
going around crying, until one
day one of them is all smiles,
introducing, buying drinks.
Had you never met one,
these nevertheless would be known
to you readily by their descriptions,
these humans, heads, legs
and arms inexplicable, graduating
immaculately like the small
blossoms into this faith,
that soon, soon the moon
shall descend to touch
us each deeply,
here.
      But there is a shadow
      to touch each roof
      at six-thirty in
      this country, and it comes to them
      singly, this shadow, it falls down to each
      as he opens the door of his car,
      it wholly becomes the space
      behind each door, beneath each lid, top and cover
      he has closed, and turns from now.
      The instant he ceases smiling
      at his victims and beneficiaries and closes

his mouth he is filled so with blackness
it spills behind him even
in the broad noon.
Yet as he fumbles for correct change only, and is angry,
observes the long-stemmed roses
opening in the greenhouses
in the winter, and is afraid,
you find that you love him:
see how he polishes his car
though it holds the whisper of his death, be filled
with joy as he expends
himself like a breath
into this, the loveliest of air,
climbing into that instrument that goes quietly,
driven by bright fire.

The Two

The airplane is like silver
that bears the two of them
to Mexico under the sun

to be divorced. Disembarking
they begin to bicker
over small matters: She

wants to be divorced
in the morning, refreshed,
but he says forget all about

the morning, I want to do it now.
You cheap, continually drowning me,
she says, by God

I want a divorce. He says fine,
you've got it: right now.
She replies she would like to wait

till morning. This goes on.
The two work their hatred
till it is like a star reduced

to the dimensions of a jewel.
The airport is quiet. The janitor's
broom whispers to the floor,

the day talks to the night,
saying just what the ocean says
to the land, what the blood

is saying to the heart,
contained, but coming, going.

Looking Out the Window Poem

The sounds of traffic
die over the back lawn
to occur again in the low
distance.

The voices, risen, of
the neighborhood cannot
maintain that pitch
and fail briefly, start
up again.

Similarly my breathing rises
and falls while I look out
the window of apartment
number three in this slum,
hoping for rage, or sorrow.

They don't come to me
anymore. How can I lament
anything? It is all
so proper, so much
as it should be, now

the nearing cumulus
clouds, ominous,
shift, they are like the
curtains, billowy,
veering at the apex
of their intrusion on the room.
If I am alive now,
it is only

to be in all this
making all possible.
I am glad to be
finally a part
of such machinery. I was
after all not so fond
of living, and there comes
into me, when I see
how little I liked
being a man, a great joy.

Look out our astounding
clear windows before evening.
It is almost as if
the world were blue
with some lubricant,
it shines so.

There Are Trains Which Will Not Be Missed

They tell you if you write great poems
you will be lifted into the clouds
like a leaf which did not know

this was possible, you will never
hear of your darkness
again, it will become
distant while you become
holy, look,

they say, at the emptiness
of train tracks and it is poetry
growing up like flowers between
the ties, but those

who say this
are not in control of themselves
or of anything and they must

lie to you in order
that they may at night not bear witness
to such great distances cascading and such

eternities unwinding
around them as to cause even the most powerful
of beds to become silences, it

is death which continues
over these chasms and these
distances deliberately like a train.

Commuting

We understand well that we must hold
our lives up in our arms like the victims
of solitary, terrible accidents,
that we must still hold our lives to their promises

and hold ourselves up to our lives
to be sure always they are larger,
wholer, realer than we ourselves, though we
must carry them.
We on this train with our lives in our laps

are waiting patiently for the next moment
and maybe we will be lifted away by our lives
as are the moments we rise up to hold with us,
or maybe we will just slacken
above our drinks in the club car chatting baseball,
all of us headed
to apply for the same job, all of us qualified,

all of us turning now into snowflakes
too delicate,
yet each holding in itself a tiny
stark particle of darkness
and weight, the heart's cinder
turning over.

Employment in the Small Bookstore

The dust almost motionless
in this narrowness, this stillness,
yet how unlike a coffin
it is, sometimes letting a live one in,
sometimes out
        and the air,
though paused, impends not a thing,
the silence isn't sinister,
and in fact not much goes on
at the Ariel Book Shop today,
no one weeps in the back
room full of books, old books, no one
is tearing the books to shreds, in fact
I am merely sitting here
talking to no one, no one being here,
and I am blameless.
        More,
I am grateful for the job,
I am fond of the books and touch them,
I am grateful that King St. goes down
to the river, and that the rain
is lovely, the afternoon green.
If the soft falling away of the afternoon
is all there is, it is nearly
enough, just
        let me hear the beautiful clear voice
of a woman in song passing
toward silence, and then
that will be all for me
at five o'clock.
        I will walk

down to see the untended
sailing yachts of the Potomac
bobbing hopelessly in another silence,
the small silence that gets to be a long
one when the past stops talking
to you because it is dead,
                              and still you listen,
hearing just the tiny
agonies of old boats
on a cloudy day, in cloudy water.
Talk to it. Men are talking to it
by Cape Charles, for them it's the same
silence with fishing lines in their hands.
We are all looking at the river bearing the wreckage
so far away. We wonder how
the river ever came to be so
gray, and think that once there were
some very big doings on this river,
and now that is all over.

Working Outside at Night

The moon swells
and its yellow darkens
nearer the horizon
and soon all
the aluminum rooftops

shall appear, orange
and distinct beside
the orange sun,
while the diamond
flares in its vacuum

within. It is simple
to be with the shovel,
thoughtless, inhabited
by this divorce,
it is good

the luminous
machinery, silenced,
waits, nice
that the conveyor
belts choked with sand

convey nothing.
When I return home to
coffee at
7:45 the lithe
young girls will be going
to high school, pulling

to their mouths stark
cigarettes through
Arizona's sunlight.
These last few months
have been awful, and when

around five the roosters
alone on neighboring
small farms begin
to scream like humans
my heart just lies down,
a stone.

An Inner Weather

This is the middle of the night.
There are no stars. It's been lightly snowing
a while, and it is silent. Many men are sleepless,
and for some, within, it is blazing noon.
The commandor cries in the street dirt,
the apprentice rides on the mayor.
And yet one pool of light
is succeeded by another tonight,
as always, amid silence, beneath the lamps,
but even these impenetrable things
waver, and aren't quite real,
and we take no comfort from them.
For the fathers parade as leering women,
the entrails of pets drape the sewer-grates.
Our shadows are black stumps.
Some of us fire
with our mouths open,
amazed, firing.
The cup is overturned by the dagger
and blood dots the window-glass.
This is the way of it
for many men this quiet night of snow.
The snow descends in a sparkling light but many are blind,
walking out without jackets as if into the sun,
and they would not say anything of the snow,
but would say only this
of the weather, that something falling burns on them.

The Supermarkets of Los Angeles

The supermarkets
of Los Angeles are blinding,
they are never closed,

they are defended
by the mountains
on the North, on

the Southeast by the
desert and on
the West by the large,

sad Pacific Ocean.

      • • •

We enter such
brilliance as we entered
the world, without

shopping list, perfectly.
It is unpleasant,
but each is thinking

he may be here
to escape still worse.
What? There is nothing

out there other
than late winter,
Hollywood, the moments

before morning.

• • •

We are never alone
here: above our heads, though
close enough nearly

to touch, is television,
in which may be disclosed
our own faces. They do not

become us. They are
the little faces we wore
as children, now wrinkled,

as if we were not grown
but only aged. We want
to cleanse those wrinkles

of accumulate filth,
these faces whose names
are being withheld, so tiny

in the relaxed fist of
Los Angeles, hearing
Los Angeles singing

to the murdered. We see
the eyes, and we see
what the eyes see,

we see the mouths moving
in utter silence, but of
course we know exactly

what the mouths are saying.

70   DENIS JOHNSON

"This Is Thursday. Your Exam Was Tuesday."

It is a fine, beautiful
and lovely time of warm dusk,
having perhaps just a touch
too much

enveloping damp;
but nice, with its idle strollers,
of whom I am one,
and it's true,
their capacity for good

is limitless, you can tell.
And then—ascending
over the roofs, the budded tips
of trees, in the twilight, very whole
and official,
its black
markings like a face

that has loomed in every city
I have known—it arrives,
the gigantic yellow warrant
for my arrest,
one sixth the size
of the world. I'm speaking
of the moon. I would not give
you a fistful of earth for
the entire moon, I might as well tell you.

For across the futile and empty
street, in the excruciating

gymnasium, they
are commencing—
degrees are being bestowed
on the deserving,
whereas I'm the incalculable

dullard in the teeshirt here.
Gentlemen of the moon:
I don't even have
my real shoes on. These are some reformed
hoodlum's shoes, from the Goodwill. Let

me rest, let me rest in the wake
of others' steady progress,
closing my eyes,
closing my heart,

shutting the door
in face after face
that has nourished me.

Falling

There is a part
of this poem where you must
say it with me, so
be ready, together we will make
it truthful, as there is gracefulness
even in the motioning of those
leafless trees, even in

such motion as descent. Fired,
I move downward through it all again
in an aquarium of debt, submerging
with the flowering electric
company, with March the 10th, 1971,
its darkness, justice and mercy

like clownfish, funnily striped.
Let them both as a matter of policy
redevour the light that
escapes them, Shakespeare
had just candles, lamps,

Milton had only the
dark, and what difference? as
poetry, like failure, is fathered
in any intensity of light, and light
in all thicknesses of darkness,

as your voice, you out there,
wakes now, please, to say
it with me: There
are descents more final, less graceful

than this plummeting
from employment; it is the middle of a false

thaw, the ice undercoating
of a bare branch is
in the midst of falling. Where
can it all be put except
in this poem, under us, breaking this fall,
itself falling
while breaking it? Look
at this line, stretching out, breaking even as it
falls to this next, like a suicide,
the weather singing
past his face, and arising to kill him
this first last line in weeks.

Students

They hold out their hands crushed
by misfortunes and I kiss
my fingers, touch my lips.

When they talk I can't help it,
I recede,
the words fall down and break.
I shut all the windows of my house
and look out onto the green lawn and am ashamed.

Students, for me, life
is just the ice-pick lying
beside the letter from the County Clerk
of Court, and the hesitation
of a hand between them,
hand I can't get
my own hand out of.
And the world—it's merely this place

of unfair vending machines
and women with short hair dyed red
who order another, and weep, and are unmasked.

Then later the world
is a repetitive street.
The hour is too late,
all, all is closed.
The red-haired woman touches the single
discolored tile in the bathroom.

She touches the marks the elastic

makes on her belly, her shoes awry.
She journeys
into the vast bed.
She reaches to the lamp
and makes it dark, relaxing.
She is not rising or even moving
but like many people at the verge of the dream
she feels as though she begins, now, to fly.

What This Window Opens On

Several of those faces on the avenue
are blossoming
into that light thrown always toward them
off the interminable, blue

backstretches
they gaze upon hopefully.
And from what separate, enraged oceans
can they possibly expect

to save themselves,
and for what? At times I say, obviously
this window opens
upon the seas and the blindnesses, it is from

this very window
that the signal will at last be issued for
the taking of our own lives.
Other times I suspect

that among the trembling inner organs
of a captured bird, people
are climbing into buses in the morning fog,
and I observe

a woman, how the movements of her parts
conspire to propel her
from grayness into grayness, vague
injustices attending her
steps until I wonder
what

can they possibly mean, down there,

by their arms and legs?—
until I wonder
what the voices must mean when they are singing.

THE
INCOGNITO
LOUNGE

O N E

The Incognito Lounge

The manager lady of this
apartment dwelling has a face
like a baseball with glasses and pathetically
repeats herself. The man next door
has a dog with a face that talks
of stupidity to the night, the swimming pool
has an empty, empty face.
My neighbor has his underwear on
tonight, standing among the parking spaces
advising his friend never to show
his face around here again.
I go everywhere with my eyes closed and two
eyeballs painted on my face. There is a woman
across the court with no face at all.

• • •

They're perfectly visible this evening,
about as unobtrusive as a storm of meteors,
these questions of happiness
plaguing the world.
My neighbor has sent his child to Utah
to be raised by the relatives of friends.
He's out on the generous lawn
again, looking like he's made
out of phosphorus.

• • •

The manager lady has just returned
from the nearby graveyard, the last
ceremony for a crushed paramedic.
All day, news helicopters cruised aloft
going whatwhatwhatwhatwhat.
She pours me some boiled
coffee that tastes like noise,
warning me, once and for all,
to pack up my troubles in an old kit bag
and weep until the stones float away.
How will I ever be able to turn
from the window and feel love for her?—
to see her and stop seeing
this neighborhood, the towns of earth,
these tables at which the saints
sit down to the meal of temptations?

• • •

And so on—nap, soup, window,
say a few words into the telephone,
smaller and smaller words.
Some TV or maybe, I don't know, a brisk
rubber with cards nobody knows
how many there are of.
Couple of miserable gerbils
in a tiny white cage, hysterical
friends rodomontading about goals
as if having them liquefied death.
Maybe invite the lady with no face
over here to explain all these elections:
life. Liberty. Pursuit.

• • •

Maybe invite the lady with no face

over here to read my palm,
sit out on the porch here in Arizona
while she touches me.
Last night, some kind
of alarm went off up the street
that nobody responded to.
Small darling, it rang for you.
Everything suffers invisibly,
nothing is possible, in your face.

• • •

The center of the world is closed.
The Beehive, the 8-Ball, the Yo-Yo,
the Granite and the Lightning and the Melody.
Only the Incognito Lounge is open.
My neighbor arrives.
They have the television on.

It's a show about
my neighbor in a loneliness, a light,
walking the hour when every bed is a mouth.
Alleys of dark trash, exhaustion
shaped into residences—and what are the dogs
so sure of that they shout like citizens
driven from their minds in a stadium?
In his fist he holds a note
in his own handwriting,
the same message everyone carries
from place to place in the secret night,
the one that nobody asks you for
when you finally arrive, and the faces
turn to you playing the national anthem
and go blank, that's
what the show is about, that message.

• • •

I was raised up from tiny
childhood in those purple hills,
right slam on the brink of language,
and I claim it's just as if
you can't do anything to this moment,
that's how inextinguishable
it all is. Sunset,
Arizona, everybody waiting
to get arrested, all very
much an honor, I assure you.
Maybe invite the lady with no face
to plead my cause, to get
me off the hook or name
me one good reason.
The air is full of megawatts

and the megawatts are full of silence.
She reaches to the radio like St. Theresa.

• • •

Here at the center of the world
each wonderful store cherishes
in its mind undeflowerable
mannequins in a pale, electric light.
The parking lot is full,
everyone having the same dream
of shopping and shopping
through an afternoon
that changes like a face.

But these shoppers of America—
carrying their hearts toward the bluffs
of the counters like thoughtless purchases,
walking home under the sea,
standing in a dark house at midnight

before the open refrigerator, completely
transformed in the light . . .

                    • • •

Every bus ride is like this one,
in the back the same two uniformed boy scouts
de-pantsing a little girl, up front
the woman whose mission is to tell the driver
over and over to shut up.
Maybe you permit yourself to find
it beautiful on this bus as it wafts
like a dirigible toward suburbia
over a continent of saloons,
over the robot desert that now turns
purple and comes slowly through the dust.
This is the moment you'll seek
the words for over the imitation
and actual wood of successive
tabletops indefatigably,
when you watched a baby child
catch a bee against the tinted glass
and were married to a deep
comprehension and terror.

White, White Collars

We work in this building and we are hideous
in the fluorescent light, you know our clothes
woke up this morning and swallowed us like jewels
and ride up and down the elevators, filled with us,
turning and returning like the spray of light that goes
around dance-halls among the dancing fools.
My office smells like a theory, but here one weeps
to see the goodness of the world laid bare
and rising with the government on its lips,
the alphabet congealing in the air
around our heads. But in my belly's flames
someone is dancing, calling me by many names
that are secret and filled with light and rise
and break, and I see my previous lives.

Enough

The terminal flopped out
around us like a dirty hankie,
surrounded by the future population
of death row in their disguises—high
school truant, bewildered Korean refugee—
we complain that Bus 18 will never arrive,
when it arrives complain what an injury
is this bus again today, venerable
and destined to stall. When it stalls

at 16th and McDowell most of us get out
to eat ourselves alive in a 24-hour diner
that promises not to carry us beyond
this angry dream of grease and the cries
of spoons, that swears our homes
are invisible and we never lived in them,
that a bus hasn't passed here in years.
Sometimes the closest I get to loving

the others is hating all of us
for drinking coffee in this stationary sadness
where nobody's dull venereal joking breaks
into words that say it for the last time,
as if we held in the heavens of our arms
not cherishable things, but only the strength
it takes to leave home and then go back again.

Night

I am looking out over
the bay at sundown and getting
lushed with a fifty-nine-
year-old heavily rouged cocktail
lounge singer, this total stranger.
We watch the pitiful little
ferry boats that ply between this world
and that other one touched
to flame by the sunset,
talking with unmanageable
excitement about the weather.
The sky and huge waters turn
vermilion as the cheap-drink hour ends.
We part with a grief as cutting
as that line between water and air.
I go downstairs and I go
outside. It is like stepping into the wake
of a tactless remark, the city's stupid
chatter hurrying to cover up
the shocked lull. The moon's
mouth is moving, and I am just
leaning forward to listen
for the eventual terrible
silence when he begins,
in the tones of a saddened
delinquent son returned
unrecognizable, naming
those things it now seems
I might have done
to have prevented his miserable
life. I am desolate.
What is happening to me.

Heat

Here in the electric dusk your naked lover
tips the glass high and the ice cubes fall against her teeth.
It's beautiful Susan, her hair sticky with gin,
Our Lady of Wet Glass-Rings on the Album Cover,
streaming with hatred in the heat
as the record falls and the snake-band chords begin
to break like terrible news from the Rolling Stones,
and such a last light—full of spheres and zones.
August,
           you're just an erotic hallucination,
just so much feverishly produced kazoo music,
are you serious?—this large oven impersonating night,
this exhaustion mutilated to resemble passion,
the bogus moon of tenderness and magic
you hold out to each prisoner like a cup of light?

The Boarding

One of these days under the white
clouds onto the white
lines of the goddamn PED
X-ING I shall be flattened,
and I shall spill my bag of discount
medicines upon the avenue,
and an abruptly materializing bouquet
of bums, retirees, and Mexican
street-gangers will see all what
kinds of diseases are enjoying me
and what kind of underwear and my little
old lady's legs spidery with veins.
So Mr. Young and Lovely Negro Bus
Driver I care exactly this: zero,
that you see these things
now as I fling my shopping
up by your seat, putting
this left-hand foot way up
on the step so this dress rides up,
grabbing this metal pole like
a beam of silver falling down
from Heaven to my aid, thank-you,
hollering, "Watch det my medicine
one second for me will you dolling,
I'm four feet and det's a tall bus
you got and it's hot and I got
every disease they are making
these days, my God, Jesus Christ,
I'm telling you out of my soul."

The Song

The small, high wailing
that envelops us here,
distant, indistinct,

yet, too, immediate,
we take to be only
the utterances of loose fan

belts in the refrigerating
system, or the shocked hum
that issues from the darkness

of telephone receivers;
but it speaks to us
so deeply we think it

may well be the beseeching
of the stars, the shameless
weeping of coyotes

out on the Mohave.
Please.
Please, stop listening

to this sound, which
is actually the terrible
keening of the ones

whose hearts have been broken
by lives spent in search
of its source,

by our lives of failure,
spent looking everywhere
for someone to say these words.

The White Fires of Venus

We mourn this senseless planet of regret,
droughts, rust, rain, cadavers
that can't tell us, but I promise
you one day the white fires
of Venus shall rage: the dead,
feeling that power, shall be lifted, and each
of us will have his resurrected one to tell him,
"Greetings. You will recover
or die. The simple cure
for everything is to destroy
all the stethoscopes that will transmit
silence occasionally. The remedy for loneliness
is in learning to admit
solitude as one admits
the bayonet: gracefully,
now that already
it pierces the heart.
Living one: you move among many
dancers and don't know which
you are the shadow of;
you want to kiss your own face in the mirror
but do not approach,
knowing you must not touch one
like that. Living
one, while Venus flares
O set the cereal afire,
O the refrigerator harboring things
that live on into death unchanged."

They know all about us on Andromeda,
they peek at us, they see us

in this world illumined and pasteled
phonily like a bus station,
they are with us when the streets fall down fraught
with laundromats and each of us
closes himself in his small
San Francisco without recourse.
They see you with your face of fingerprints
carrying your instructions in gloved hands
trying to touch things, and know you
for one despairing, trying to touch the curtains,
trying to get your reflection mired in alarm tape
past the window of this then that dark
closed business establishment.
The Andromedans hear your voice like distant amusement park
    music
converged on by ambulance sirens
and they understand everything.
They're on your side. They forgive you.

I want to turn for a moment to those my heart loves,
who are as diamonds to the Andromedans,
who shimmer for them, lovely and useless, like diamonds:
namely, those who take their meals at soda fountains,
their expressions lodged among the drugs
and sunglasses, each gazing down too long
into the coffee as though from a ruined balcony.
O Andromedans they don't know what to do
with themselves and so they sit there
until they go home where they lie down
until they get up, and you beyond the light years know
that if sleeping is dying, then waking
is birth, and a life
is many lives. I love them because they know how
to manipulate change
in the pockets musically, these whose faces the seasons
never give a kiss, these

who are always courteous to the faces
of presumptions, the presuming streets,
the hotels, the presumption of rain in the streets.
I'm telling you it's cold inside the body that is not the body,
lonesome behind the face
that is certainly not the face
of the person one meant to become.

T W O

Nude

My luck has been so all but
perfect I can imagine
nothing that might be added

save perhaps one or two more
such truly astonishing
visions as these fine hairs—

blossoms, really, these little
originations of life in
the parched world, this excellent

sparse grove that is lucked on,
never sought and found, just here
above the navel, just here where

I touch for one second
and then I must recover.
Also, if my good luck is not

yet quite too far beyond
that prudently afforded
my sort, I would like

to have several more
of these buttocks, precisely
duplicated, naturally

presenting as it fades this pale
impression of my fingers
on the left one. And may I have

the bodies with them, too? This
is actually the most unnerving
and celestial of girls, it's

not enough that she was in
the living room now as I entered,
why couldn't she have been in

the room I just left, as well
as all the other rooms at once?
Do you see what foul lurches

underproduction leaves us in?
And so suppose this girl were
to become lost? Lost! Would you

want to witness my running
into all the rooms exclaiming
year after year Whatever

shall I do? Lately I have been
noticing how everything
loved must reach the touch

of grief to the lover—it is
an unusual prize geranium
that does not die—but perhaps

one or two more of this girl,
of course with these arresting—
oh, my, these prosecuting

and sentencing!—thin arms,
each finely braceleted or
just plain covered with twenty-

dollar bills, emeralds, alarm
devices and this bewildering
soft skin could be managed?

Vespers

The towels rot and disgust me on this damp
peninsula where they invented mist
and drug abuse and taught the light to fade,
where my top-quality and rock-bottom heart
cries because I'll never get to kiss
your famous knees again in a room made
vague by throwing a scarf over a lamp.
Things get pretty radical in the dark:
the sailboats on the inlet sail away;
the provinces of actuality
crawl on the sea; the dusk now tenderly
ministers to the fallen parking lots—
the sunset instantaneous on the fenders,
memory and peace . . . the grip of chaos . . .

The Story

Dunking one
adjacent a disturbed
old woman in the elevated
train station donut shop,
you think: Heavenly lady,

I'm drinking coffee
and you're dripping mucus,
is that the story?—but say nothing,
fearing either reply. Curious
days, these, spent

in fear of replies, in horror
of doorways, sleep, friendships,
and what napkins!—wordless
white interrogations wanting
the whole story, again,

from the beginning;
napkins like the vast, anemic
dawns that find you awake
by the window, trying to
remember how it goes,

failing: the disastrously loved
one's face some Martian's
now, the swell architecture of the old
houses similarly permutating
in memory's half-light,
and boxes?—What
can you do save drift

motherless through these tears when
the cardboard box remembers
the legend of the distant

store in a cool dry place
where all are freed of desire
and change, the fat man
simply standing, selling
nothing, the others silent,

every edge gleaming
with the perfect, acrylic veneer
of reality? But does a box
dream, or is it you who dreams,
and is this truly a dream of reality

or only a memory of sanity?
Turn around. Look back. Now
remember: there they drank wine
with you a last time,
there they cried with you a last time,

now the shelter is only a hailstone
that fell there,
for already they've folded away the voices,
already they've put away the light,
now that this one
whom we told
nothing
goes away saying I hear your words,
I will seek these things,
I will know by these signs.

Surreptitious Kissing

I want to say that
forgiveness keeps on

dividing, that hope
gives issue to hope,

and more, but of course I
am saying what is

said when in this dark
hallway one encounters

you, and paws and
assaults you—love

affairs, fast lies—and you
say it back and we

blunder deeper, as would
any pair of loosed

marionettes, any couple
of cadavers cut lately

from the scaffold,
in the secluded hallways

of whatever is
holding us up now.

From a Berkeley Notebook

One changes so much
from moment to moment
that when one hugs
oneself against the chill
air at the inception
of spring, at night,
knees drawn to chin,
he finds himself in the arms
of a total stranger,
the arms of one he might move
away from on the dark playground.

Also, it breaks the heart
that the sign revolving like
a flame above the gas
station remembers the price
of gas, but forgets entirely
this face it has been
looking at all day.
And so the heart is exhausted
that even in the face

of the dismal facts we wait
for the loves of the past
to come walking from the fire,
the tree, the stone, tangible
and unchanged and repentant
but what can you do.
Half the time I think
about my wife and child,
the other half I think how

to become a citizen

with an apartment, and sex
too is quite on my mind,
though it seems the women
have no time for you here,
for which in my larger, more
mature moments I can't blame them.
These are the absolute

pastures I am led to:
I am in Berkeley, California,
trapped inside my body,
I am the secret my body
is going to keep forever,
as if its secret were
merely silence. It lies
between two mistakes
of the earth,

the San Andreas
and Hayward faults,
and at night from
the hill above the stadium
where I sleep,
I can see the yellow
aurora of Telegraph
Avenue uplifted

by the holocaust.
My sleeping
bag has little
cowboys lassoing bulls
embroidered all over
its pastel inner
lining, the pines are tall

and straight, converging
in a sort of roof

above me, it's nice,
oh loves, oh loves, why
aren't you here? Morgan,
the pyjamas are so
lonesome without
the orangutans—I write
and write, and transcend
nothing, escape
nothing, nothing
is truly born from me,
yet magically it's better
than nothing—I know

you must be quite
changed by now, but you
are just the same, too,
like those stars that keep
shining for a long time after
they go out—but it's just a light
they touch us with this
evening amid the fine
rain like mist, among the pines.

On the Olympic Peninsula

Stranger, to one like you,
here only the old
people feel like talking—
but abruptly, as if already in the midst
of talk, as if they sensed
with you a kinship in closeness
to endings—and you aren't kind
with them. Stranger,
here the sea doesn't obliterate,
but just lies there carved up
into bays and inlets, indolent
or waiting. In the town's one
hip bar the lesbians lean
into sinister embraces, dancing
together and speaking just softly
enough that you can't hear. Your girl
is gone and you are here
because you think maybe they
have taken her from you
into this establishment where the men
stink like murdered sea animals;
they have flying beards, black
mouths they spill the beer
into over their laughter
so that you think of someone urinating on coals.
Sometimes you unexpectedly taste
the inside of your own mouth, choking
as you kiss this bitter foreigner,
and you feel yourself forgetting, even as you remember,
that you've gone strange and everybody
else is happy and just having

good clean fun in a place where the ocean
is large and cares nothing for men,
that you are an image of blood
graven amid peace and wine,
a strange one,
claustrophobic and heart-stopped among
garden parks through which boys
jog perspiring in their red basketball
shorts and in which toddlers
in blue parkas on toy horses rock themselves,
already stupefied, toward oblivion.

A Woman

There's nobody here
but you, sitting under
the window at the corner
table as if waiting
for somebody to speak,
over your left shoulder the moon,
behind your head a vagina,
in pencil, emblazoned
above a telephone number.
For two hours you've been
looking across the street,
quite hard, at the grand store,
the Shopper's Holiday felled
across the sunset.
It grows dark in this climate
swiftly: the night
is as sudden and vacuous
as the paper sack the attendant
balloons open with a shake
of his scarred wrist,
and in the orange parking
lot's blaze of sulphur
arc lamps, each fist
of tissue paper is distinct,
all cellophane edged
with a fiery light that seems
the white heat of permanence
and worth; of reality;
at this hour, and in this
climate where how swiftly
the dark grows, and the time comes.

Now

Whatever the foghorns are
the voices of feels terrible
tonight, just terrible, and here
by the window that looks out
on the waters but is blind, I
have been sleeping,
but I am awake now.
In the night I watch
how the little lights
of boats come out
to us and are lost again
in the fog wallowing on the sea:
it is as if in that absence not many
but a single light gestures
and diminishes like meaning
through speech, negligently
adance to the calling
of the foghorns like the one
note they lend from voice
to voice. And so does my life tremble,
and when I turn from the window
and from the sea's grief, the room
fills with a dark
lushness and foliage nobody
will ever be plucked from,
and the feelings I have
must never be given speech.
Darkness, my name is Denis Johnson,
and I am almost ready to
confess it is not some awful
misunderstanding that has carried

me here, my arms full of the ghosts
of flowers, to kneel at your feet;
almost ready to see
how at each turning I chose
this way, this place and this verging
of ocean on earth with the horns claiming
I can keep on if only I step
where I cannot breathe. My coat
is leprosy and my dagger
is a lie; must I
shed them? Do I have
to end my life in order
to begin? Music, you are light.
Agony, you are only what tips
me from moment to moment, light
to light and word to word,
and I am here at the waters
because in this space between spaces
where nothing speaks,
I am what it says.

T H R E E

Ten Months After Turning Thirty

We've been to see a movie, a rotten one
that cost four dollars, and now we slip
in a cheap car along expensive streets
through a night broken open like a stalk
and offering up a sticky, essential darkness,
just as the terrible thing inside of me,
the thick green vein of desire or whatever it was,
is broken and I can rest.
Maybe in another place and time, people
drive slowly past the taverns
with black revolvers reaching from their windows,
but here in the part of night where every
breath is a gift tremendous as the sea,
thousands of oleanders wave
blossoms like virgins after a war.
I can hear my own scared laughter coming back
from desolate rooms where the light-bulbs
lunge above the radios all night,
and I apologize now to those
rooms for having lived in them. Things
staggered sideways a while. Suddenly
I'm stretched enough to call certain of my days
the old days, remembering how we burned
to hear of the destruction of the world,

how we hoped for it until many of us were dead,
the most were lost, and a couple lucky
enough to stand terrified outside the walls
of Jerusalem knowing things we never learned.

In a Light of Other Lives

It's raining, and the streetlights on the wet
street are like regurgitated lights,
but the ambulance's ruby element
can move among our rooms without a care,
so that we who generally sleep
where it is black awaken in a red
light of other lives, saying I
can see every article,
I can see every article in its fame.
Saying How long do I stay here in the jail
of times like this, where the clear
water has the flavor of thirst
and the meat tastes like it is eating me
and the day's bread changes into a face?
Where sometimes you see the sorrow of a whole life
open away from you white as an invitation
on the blue of night, and the moon is a monster?
All the night long I can betray myself in the honky-tonk
of terror and delight, I can throw away my faith,
go loose in the spectacular fandango
of emergencies that strum the heart
with neon, but I can't
understand anything. It is coming:
the curtains of rain and light the arc lamps
let down on First Avenue will be parted,
and from behind them, the people we really are will step out
with abandon, as if asked to dance—
the myriad tickets will fall away from the face
and the visions of the heart be delivered up naked
and lucid as teeth, and each
of the things that catch up with this robber

will fall on God: now *You* must follow
the spoor of Your own blood among
edifices, among monuments, until the police
have You in their arms
and make You say Your name.
I want to be there when the little pool of light
falls on the identification,
I swear I will never tell the others if You whisper
to me what this moment is before the ambulances,
and what these moments are
when all that was impending
begins, when the whole
downtown, arrested like a lung
between intake and expulsion, erupts
into genuineness—as if many
bells have been struck and what
the world is, is that I can touch
their ringing. It is unbreakable.
It is the examiner before whom the emptiness
inside me perjures itself.
It is the examiner who is a fist.

For Jane

At left, with a net, in a light
like whiskey, you skim flotsam
from the water.
I can't tell you how vivid
this undertaking is—
you are as unsettling
and as naked as that yellow
flower admiring you as it rests
along the surface of the pool.
I am just going to listen
to the sound of liquid,
the sound of oleanders.

If ever
I was about to speak I
forget. I can see
that the single flower goes
aloft on the water of
the pool because it is something
that everything has addressed
to my darling, while I stand
here like some ashes
that used to be a clown,
looking out quietly
from my face to watch the failure
of these words to be those things.

Sway

Since I find you will no longer love,
from bar to bar in terror I shall move
past Forty-third and Halsted, Twenty-fourth
and Roosevelt where fire-gutted cars,
their bones the bones of coyote and hyena,
suffer the light from the wrestling arena
to fall all over them. And what they say
blends in the tarantellasmic sway
of all of us between the two of these:
harmony and divergence,
their sad story of harmony and divergence,
the story that begins
I did not know who she was
and ends *I did not know who she was.*

The Circle

for Jane, after a dream

I passed a helicopter
crashed in the street today,
where stunned and suddenly grief-torn
passers-by tried to explain
over and over, a hundred ways, what
had happened. Some cried over the pilot,
others stole money from his wallet—
I heard the one responsible for his death
claiming the pilot didn't need it any more,
and whether he spoke of the pilot's
money or his life wasn't clear.
The scene had a subaqueous timbre
that I recognize now as a light
that shines in the dreams I have when I sleep
on my back and wake up half-drowned.
However I tried to circumnavigate
this circus of fire and mourning—
the machine burst ajar like a bug,
the corpse a lunch pail
left open and silly music coming out—
I couldn't seem to find a way
that didn't lead straight to the heart of the trouble
and involve me forever in their grief.

The Woman in the Moon

for Glenna K., 1922–1979

Who wouldn't have been afraid
of your face?—watching me
from another world through your cheap
frame on the dresser, while your daughter
wept and I made hysterical
love to her, trying
to banish your ghost that wandered
with its smashed head through this life
I never invited you to.
Who wouldn't have wanted to drive you out of her,
seeing how your memory, grown
sharp as flint in grief, carved
her face a little more every
day into yours?
I thought you were watching me out of her eyes,

I thought every night I heard the telephone
clatter to the floor again,
and your daughter
scream so she couldn't stop.
And for months afterward
you came to me like
nobody—secondhand,
through a daughter's hindsight,
her unblinking, horrified love,
as night
after night the room filled
with the dark and the air
burned with your murdered presence,

until I couldn't possibly make love to the dark gold
woman, vessel of your self, the torn
strings of your motherhood dripping
from her like an ocean
where she drowned but couldn't die.
Who would drag us before some tribe of elders
to be scorned,
or have anything but pity
on us, that we turned to other lovers
and lost each other?
Glenna,

forgive me: tonight, in a moment
of learning that is as clear
and absolute as ice, and hurts
as much to be inside of,
I see how much like him
I've become, the man
who beat you until you died with something
they never found—
walking in an anger of love
and hatred through these streets
just as the geraniums

of light around the baseball
diamonds are coming on—
oh, God, inside me I carry a black
night you climb through like
the moon in which the Asians
see a woman:
higher

and smaller, Glenna, farther
and farther away,
and nothing
will ever bring you back.
And nothing will ever get rid of you.

The Flames

In 1972 I crossed Kansas on a bus
with a dog apparently pursued to skinniness
painted on its side, an emblem
not entirely inappropriate, considering
those of us availing ourselves
of its services—tossed
like rattles in a baby's hand,
sleeping the sleep of the ashamed
and the niggardly, crying out
or keeping our counsel as we raced over the land,
flailing at dreams
or lying still. And I awoke to see
the prairie, seized by the cold and the early hour,
continually falling away beside us, and a fire
burning furiously in the dark: a house
posted about by tiny figures—
firemen; and a family
who might have been calling out to God
just then for a witness.

But more than witness, I remember now
something I could only have imagined
that night: the sound of the reins breaking
the bones in the farmer's hands
as the horses reared and flew back into the flames
he wanted to take them away from.
My thoughts are like that,
turning and going back where nothing wants them,
where the door opens and a road
of light falls through it
from behind you and pain

starts to whisper with your voice;
where you stand inside your own absence,
your eyes still smoky from dreaming,
the ruthless iron press
of love and failure making
a speechless church out of your dark
and invisible face.

F O U R

Minutes

You and I—we agitate
to say things, to dress every gash
with a street address or a relative.
We are found in the places of transport at an hour
when only the criminals are expected to depart.

We are blind and we don't know that our mouths
are moving as we place a hand to stay
the janitor's mop—*I'll tell you the story*
of my life, you'll make a million—
blind and we don't know that our parents are dead

as we enter the photo-booths.
In there is the quiet like the kernel of a word:
in there everything we were going to say
is taken from us and we are given
four images of ourselves. What are we going

to do with these pictures? They hold
no fascination for the abandoned,
but only for us, who have
relinquished them to the undertow
that held us, too, but let us go,

so that the hospitals opened like great vaults
for us and we stepped from bed to bed
on the faces of the diseased, the beloved,
moving like light over a necklace
of excruciations—*I'll tell you*

the story of my life,
you'll make a million . . .
this is what it means to be human,
to witness the heart of a moment like a photograph,
the present standing up through itself relentlessly like a fountain,

the clock showering the intersection with minutes
even as it gathers them to its face
in the so often alluded
to Kingdom of Heaven—
to watch one of those minutes open

like a locket and brandish a picture
of everyone we ever loved who drowned,
while the unendurable generosity of everything
sells everything out. Would you like
to dance? Then here, dance with the terror

that now is forever,
my feet are stumps. The band is just
outbreaking now with one that goes
all the evidence / the naughty evidence / persuades
the lovers endearing by the ponds /

the truants growing older in the sleazy arcades /
there's no banishing / of anything /
only con- / quering within /
make it enough / make it enough / or eat
suffering without end

The Coming of Age

Outside the spring
afternoon
is occurring, my love,
just as our voices
are going home from us
to the plains, and the shapes
of ourselves, as we impose
them on this one, prepare
to blend with other
afternoons, possibly in
this very room
as tiny dusts uplifted
in the bands of sunlight,
or in other still chambers.
I don't want you to be afraid
as we stand here losing
our lives, unable to speak,
soon to enter the dream
of once having touched
this portion, that smoothness
of flesh now buried dead
and having heard the lovely
tones ascending on a voice
merely speaking; there is
the chance there will be
the singing of the voiceless,
unraveling into the unenclosed
emptiness a silence
drawn taut so

124   DENIS JOHNSON

slowly its
high music encounters
us before
it begins, and we are dancing.

You

You were as blind to me
as your footprints last Friday,
but I saw you dancing
with that girl who wasn't me—
because I don't dance
and laugh in that terrible
style with every stranger.
But you are no stranger.

But you were strange when you were dancing,
and the room turned all yellow
and the glass I was holding
spilled burgundy wine.
I got out by the side door
and I leaned on a box,
and I saw you at the end
of every street,

and in the Flame Inn
I watched the men shooting
eight-ball and mule-kicking
the jukebox till it worked.
On the wall they had many,
many wooden plaques
bearing humorous sayings
that I will never say
to you even if you begged me,
not even if you came out
of a prison, and begged me.

Poem

There was something I can't bring myself
to mention in the way the light
seemed trapped by the clouds,
the way the road dropped
from pavement to dirt and the land from pine
to scrub—
the red-headed vultures on dead animals,
the hatred of the waitress breaking

a cup and kicking the shards across the café
that looked out on the mountain and on the white smear
of the copper mine that sustained these people.
I claim there was something you wouldn't
have wanted to speak of either,
a sense of some violent treasure
like uranium waiting to be romanced
out of the land . . .

They sat under white umbrellas,
two or three together, elbows on card tables
at the dirt roads leading to the mines,
rising each at his turn to walk
around a while with a sign
announcing they were on strike,
their crystalline and indelible
faces in the hundred-degree
heat like the faces of slaughtered hogs,
and God forgive me,
I pulled to the side of the road and wrote this poem.

Radio

He bears a rakish feather
through the streets in a hat
on his head and has had
several drinks, and is crying.
He totters at the change
of traffic lights.
I do not know if he has just
been orphaned, or what.
From a room above the stores
the insistent test-tone
of the Emergency Broadcasting
System stares at him, and he
cannot stop hearing it.
The perfectly desolate afternoon's
single utterance is this sound
like an ambulance across
the mild lake whose driver
swims while the siren cries.
It is putting the man
in the feathered hat at
the intersection under arrest.
I do not know if he has just
been informed, or what.
I know it is my radio, but
I am only beginning to understand
whose orphanhood, whose tears.

Tomorrow

I take
you by your arm of stained glass
while the moon turns warm and wet
as the kitchen window of a distant
restaurant in the beautiful
moments after closing,
and we walk up and down—
oh! don't we promenade?
Every radio in the town
plays the same station through doorways
thrown wide to the elements and we are
buoyed and relayed how tenderly along
this underground railroad of tuneful oldies.
It is a nighttime filled
with animals, bubbles, tiny lights.
Now we do not fear treachery,
now we are not asking ourselves how
will we know if the insect lies,
how will we know if the fire lies.
The ache of our loving just
throttles us speechless inside the midnight,
though the radios are all crying out
that the weather tomorrow in
the mountains will be unprecedented.

The Confession of
St. Jim-Ralph

Our Patron of Falling Short,
Who Became a Prayer

I used to sneak into the movies without paying.
I watched the stories but I failed to see the dark.
I went to college and drank everything they gave me,
and I never paid for any of that water
on which I drifted as if by grace until
after the drownings, when in the diamond light
of seven-something A.M., as the spring was tearing
me up in Cartajena, only praying
on my knees before the magnifying ark
of the Seventh St. Hotel could possibly save me,
until falling on my face before the daughter
of money while the world poured from the till
brought the moment's length against the moment's height,
and paying was what I was earning and eating and wearing.
This to the best of my recollection
my uncle said in 1956,
moving against my father like a bear
on fire as the evening of his visit
killed the rum. He'd come from Alaska
or some place like that, the Antarctic, maybe,
and he left in a hot rage, screaming by the door
that nothing would save me from my awful father,
just as he, my uncle, had been saved
by nothing. Thirteen weeks from then, he died.
"This family's full of the dead," my father told me.
I was eight. I used to make excuses

to join him in the washroom as he bathed
in the mornings, soaping himself carefully
so as not to splash the automatic pistol
wrapped in plastic he rested near to hand.
At a certain point, the sun came through the blinds
and shafted the toilet bowl, filling it with light
as he spoke of killing everyone, often taking
the pistol from its wrap and holding its mouth
against his breast, explaining that no safety
lay anywhere, unless he should shoot the fear
that stood up on its hind legs in his heart.
Such things were always on TV—I thought
that one world merged in the next, and I resolved
to win the great Congressional Medal of Honor,
to make a name on the stage, and die a priest.

In the war the bullets yanked the fronds
from palms and the earth ate them up like acid
before our eyes. When dead men hit the ground
they came alive, they spoke in tongues, holding
babies that came from nowhere in their arms.
We were all afraid of the earth. My father's fear
turned it like a plow, delivering
dogs and bugs, bright music, and a feminine
whispering of our names. My comrades fled,
but I was healed by everything that happened,
the midnight Rapid Transit stations
of hand grenades made moonlight as I moved
from life to life, getting off and shouting
whatever the signs said, getting on again,
received like lightning, changing everything.
My body disappeared. The enemy
knew me as a ghost who dropped a shadow
the size of night and turned the air to edges.
I am your grand companion of surprise,
big-time harbinger canceling everyone's

business in a constant dream of all
the starring roles and franchises the great
Congressional Medal of Honor winners win.
Wounded twice, then decorated more
than any other in my regiment,
I stood at home plate, vomit on my blouse
and whiskey in my blood, and heard the dirt
of my home town falling grain by grain
out of the afternoon, while everyone's
rahrahrahs affected me like silence.
The mayor handed me a four-by-four-
inch cardboard box a colonel handed *him;*
I threw it at the vast face of the crowd,
screaming I wanted only the Medal of Honor . . .
I lose the thread of my existence here.
I see me strange and drugged against my will,
telling my life story to a room,
traveling the aisles of an asylum
out there in Maine, among the aborigines.
They must have set me loose, or I escaped:
I see myself in a forest-bordered field,
unchanged and wearing my uniform—
free; yet somehow jailed by old desires
and saying what a soldier says: For home,
nothing. Comrades, for you, these hoarded rations.

With four monstrosities in uniforms
like mine, I pulverized guitars and wept
for the merriment of many. Brothers,
when shadows lengthen, and they lower down
the American flag and close our government,
another country rises like a mist
by garbagey coliseums on the warehouse
side of town to listen to that rock
and roll: God speaking with the Devil's voice,
unbreathable air of manacles, a storm

to bless your multicolored lips with sperm.
We sundered them until they brought their bones
forth from the flesh and laid them at our feet,
screaming their lungs shut tight as fists,
shedding their homes forever, leaving name
and tongue and mind and sending us their heads
through the mails in the night. We ran it past the edge,
we gave them something everyone could dance to—
whatever is most terrible is most real—
the Bible fights, the fetuses burning in light-bulbs,
the cunnilingual, intravenous
swamp of love. Three times I died on stage,
and the show went on while doctors snatched
me back from Chinatown with their machines.
We struck it rich. Without a repertoire,
without a name or theme, we toured the land
and eighty thousand perished. We were *real*,
but not one company recorded us:
everywhere we went they passed a law.
We toured the land—sweet, burning Texacos,
the adrenaline darkness palpitates frantically,
the highway eats itself all night, the radio's
wheedling bebop fails in the galactic
soup near dawn; the Winnebago shimmers,
everything tastes like puke, the eight-ball
bursts, nobody
knows how to drink in this fuckin town . . .
One night I heard our music end
abruptly in the middle of a number
and looked around me at a gigantic silence.
I felt the pounding, saw the screams, but all
was like the long erasure of a wind
calming and disturbing everything
on its route through stunned fields of hay.
My bodyguards tried with huge gentleness to lead
me off, but I threw myself outside, rolling

through a part of town I'd never seen—
the flat gray streets looked Hebrew, and the windows
held out the paraphernalia of old age,
porcelain Jesuses gesturing from the shadows
of porcelain vases, surrounded by medicines.
A rain began. I strained myself to hear
the trashcans say their miserable names,
but nothing. At the brink
of stardom high over the United States,
untouchable as God but better known,
I stumbled over streets that might've been rubber,
deaf as a cockroach, finished as a singer.

Brothers, I spilled myself along the roads.
Mold grew on me as I dampened in alleys.
I began in ignorance. How could I know
that whoever is grinding up his soul is making
himself afresh? That the ones who run away
get nearer all the time? Look here or there,
it's always the horizon, the dull edge
of earth dicing your plan like a potato.
Does water break the light, or light the water?
Which do you choose: what is or what is?
I painted myself black and let that color
ride through virgins like the penises
they dream of while their fathers sleep. I lied.
I cheated like a shark. I robbed the dead.
Nothing healed me, just as nothing healed
my uncle of himself—but he was healed,
while I grew phosphorescent with a kind
of cancer that I carried like a domino,
a tiny badge discovering me . . .
Oh please my love I want to rock and roll with you
Feel it feel it
feel it all night like a shoe . . .
Ten years I wasted all I had, and then

ten years I lived correctly—held a job
in a factory that made explosions,
where deafness was an asset. I did well,
I never missed a day, I polished late,
honed my skills, received promotions—in the end
I built explosions for atomic bombs,
forty-three I built myself, which one of these
days will deafen you, as I am deafened.
I wrenched the fraternal orders with my tale
of sorrowful delinquency—the Elks,
the Lions, Moose; those animals, they loved
the crippled rock'n'roller with the heart
wrung out as empty as his former mind,
and variously and often they cited me.
I walked the malls with an expanded chest,
took my sips with my pinkie cocked,
firing dry martinis at my larynx
and yearning for the strength of soul it takes
to suck a bullet from an actual
pistol, hating my own drained face
as I intimidated mirrors, or stood
in a jail of lies before the Eagle Scouts,
an alarm clock going off inside an alarm clock
in a lump of iron inside a lump of iron:
hating myself for having become my father.
At night I prayed aloud to God and Jesus
to place me on a spaceship to the moon—
Heaven, I told Them constantly, my mind
is tired of me, and I would like to die.
Take me to ground zero take me to ground zero
where in the midst of detonation it is useless
to demonstrate quod erat demonstrandum,
this was my ceaseless prayer, until my lips
were muscles and my heart could talk,
telling it over and over to itself;
until they fired me and drove me to the edge

of things, and dumped my prayer into the desert.
Drinking cactus milk and eating sand,
I wandered until I saw the monastery
standing higher and higher, at first a loose
mirage, but soon more real than I was.
There I fell on my face, and let light carry
me into the world—just as my uncle told it
nine million years ago when I was eight—
and the prison of my human shape exploded,
my heart cracked open and the blood poured out
over stones that got up and walked when it touched them.
High in the noon, some kind of jet plane winked
like a dime; I saw it also flashed
over the vast, perfumed, commercial places
filled with stupid but well-intentioned people,
the wreckages and ambushes of love
putting themselves across, making it pay
in the margins of the fire, in the calm spaces,
taken across the dance-floor by a last romance,
kissing softly in a hallucination strewn
with bus tickets and an originless music—
and now death comes to them, a little boy
in a baseball cap and pyjamas, doing things
to the locks of the heart . . . This was my vision.
Here I saw the truth of the horizon,
the way of coming and going in this life.
I never drifted up from my beginning:
I rose as inexorably as heat.

Brothers, I reached you, and you took me in.
You saw me when I was invisible,
you spoke to me when I was deaf,
you thanked me when I was a secret,
and how will I make of myself something
at this hour when I am already made?
Never a famous hero, a star, a priest—

my mind decides a little faster than
the world can talk, and what I dreamed was only
the darker sketch of what I would become.
It's 1996. I'm forty-eight.
I am a monk who never prays. I am
a prayer. The pilgrim comes to hear me;
the banker comes, the bald janitors arrive,
the mothers lift their wicked children up—
they wait for me as if I were a bus,
with or without hope, what's the difference?
One guy manipulates a little calculator,
speaking to it as to a friend. Sweat
is delivered from its mascara,
sad women read about houses . . .
and now the deaf approach, trailing the dark smoke
of their infirmity behind them as they leave it
and move toward the prayer that everything
is praying: the summer evening a held bubble,
every gesture riveting the love,
the swaying of waitresses, the eleven television
sets in a storefront broadcasting a murderer's face—
these things speak the clear promise of Heaven.

Passengers

The world will burst like an intestine in the sun,
the dark turn to granite and the granite to a name,
but there will always be somebody riding the bus
through these intersections strewn with broken glass
among speechless women beating their little ones,
always a slow alphabet of rain
speaking of drifting and perishing to the air,
always these definite jails of light in the sky
at the wedding of this clarity and this storm
and a woman's turning—her languid flight of hair
traveling through frame after frame of memory
where the past turns, its face sparking like emery,
to open its grace and incredible harm
over my life, and I will never die.

THE
VEIL

O N E

The Rockefeller Collection of Primitive Art

Solter my neighbor rocks his lover through the human night,
softly and softly, so as not to tell the walls,
the walls the friends of the spinster. But I'm only a spinster,
I'm not a virgin. I have made love. I have known desire.

I followed desire through the museums.
We seemed to float along sculptures,
along the clicking ascent
of numerals in the guards' hands. Brave works
by great masters were all around us.

And then we came out of a tunnel into one of those restaurants
where the natural light was so unnatural
as to make heavenly even our fingernails and each radish.
I saw everyone's skull beneath the skin,
I saw sorrow painting its way out of the faces,
someone was telling a lie and I could taste it,
and I heard the criminal tear-fall,
saw the dog
who dances with his shirt rolled up to his nipples,
the spider . . .

Why are their mouths small tight circles,
the figures of Africa, New Guinea, New Zealand,

why are their mouths astonished kisses beneath drugged eyes,
why is the eye of the cantaloupe expressionless
but its skin rippling with terror,
and out beyond Coney Island in the breathless waste
of Atlantia, why
does the water move when it is already there?
My neighbor's bedsprings struggle
—soon she will begin to scream—

I think of them always
traveling through space,
riding their bed so
softly it staves the world through the air

of my room—it is their right,
because we freely admit how powerful the sight is,
we say that eyes stab and glances rake,
but it is not the sight
that lets us taste the salt on someone's shoulder in the night,
the musk of fear in the morning,
the savor of falling in the falling
elevators in the buildings of rock,
it is the dark that lets us it is the dark. If
I can imagine them then
why can't I imagine this?

Talking Richard Wilson Blues, by Richard Clay Wilson

You might as well take a razor
to your pecker as let a woman in your heart.
First they do the wash and then they kill you.
They flash their lights and teach your wallet to puke.
They bring it to you folded—if you see her
stepping between the coin laundry and your building
over the slushy street and watch the clothing steam,
you can't wait to open up the door when she puts
the stairs behind her and catch that warmth between you.
It changes into a baby. "Here's to the little shitter,
the little linoleum lizard." Once he peed on me
when I was changing him—that one got a laugh
from the characters I wasted all my chances with
at Popeye's establishment when it was over
by the Wonderland. But it's destroyed
now and I understand one of those shopping malls
that are like great monuments of blindness
and folly stands there. And next door,
the grimy restaurants of men with movies
where they used to wear human faces,
the sad people from space. But that was never me,
because everything in those days depended on my work.
"Listen, I'm going to work," was all I could say,
and drunk or sober I would put on the uniform
of Texaco and wade into my life.
I felt like a man of honor and substance,
but the situation was dancing underneath me—
once I walked into the living room at my sister's
and saw that the two of them, her and my sister,
had turned sometime behind my back not exactly
fatter, but heavy, or squalid, with cartoons

moving across the television in front of them,
surrounded by laundry, and a couple of Coca-Colas
standing up next to the iron on the board.
I stepped out into the yard of bricks
and trash and watched the light light
up the blood inside each leaf,
and I asked myself, Now what is the rpm
on this mother? Where do you turn it on?
I think you understand how I felt.
I'm not saying everything changed in the space
of one second of seeing two women, but I did
start dragging her into the clubs with me. I insisted
she be sexy. I just wanted to live.
And I did: some nights were so
sensory I felt the starlight landing on my back
and I believed I could set fire to things with my fingers—
but the strategies of others broke my promise.
At closing time once, she kept talking to a man
when I was trying to catch her attention to leave.
It was a Negro man, and I thought of black limousines
and black masses and black hydrants filled
with black water. When the lights came on
you could see all kinds of intentions in the air.
I thought I might smack her face, or spill a glass,
but instead I opened him up with my red fishing knife
and I took out his guts and I said, "Here they are,
motherfucker, nigger, here they are."
There were people frozen around us. The lights had just come on.
At that moment I saw her reading me and reading me
from the end of the world where I saw her standing,
and the way the sacred light played across her face
all I can tell you is I had to be a diamond
of ice to manage. Right down the middle from beginning to end
my life pours into one ocean: into this prison
with its empty ballfield and its empty
preparations for Never Happen.

If she ever comes to visit me, to hell with her,
I won't talk to her, and my son can entertain
himself. God kill them both. I'm sorry for nothing.
I'm just an alien from another planet.
I am not happy. Disappointment
lights its stupid fire in my heart,
but two days a week I staff
the Max Security laundry above the world
on the seventh level, looking at two long roads
out there that go to a couple of towns.
Young girls accelerating through the intersection
make me want to live forever,
they make me think of the grand things,
of wars and extremely white, quiet light that never dies.
Sometimes I stand against the window for hours
tuned to every station at once, so loaded on crystal
meth I believe I'll drift out of my body.
Jesus Christ, your doors close and open,
you touch the maniac drifters, the fireaters,
I could say a million things about you
and never get that silence out of time
that happens when the blank muscle hangs
between its beats—that is what I mean
by darkness, the place where I kiss your mouth,
where nothing bad has happened.
I'm not anyone but I wish I could be told
when you will come to save us. I have written
several poems and several hymns, and one
has been performed on the religious
ultrahigh frequency station. And it goes like this.

The Skewbald Horse

I wish to tell about a time
That's gone,
When I looked at the wheat and thought it was the sea.
I rode to town. The light was gold. I heard them
Speak of the future—around them the dogs dreamed.
It was Sunday, and in our town
The church bells then were so arranged
As to play "Amazing Grace" upon the drugged
Air and clenched hearts of August. And all the time
The wheat in its inlets of honey
Perished and replaced itself imperceptibly
And the horses swam slowly through the fields.
I breathed something thick and terrible,
Riding home toward the falling sun, a wild
Musical heat of sorrow and youth that made
A great strength up and down me. I
Was desire—what lived in the sad, slow
Thighs of young girls the dull breeze
Pressed their aprons to embrace? The same
Pitchblende dying between mine? Whatever
It was, I believed it whirled the Earth,
In faith and troth, whatever it was—
Mingling of phosphor and lodestone
Drawn through our hearts—caught fire,
And didn't it ride the horse and me, but we
Rode through it also? All
Were in town: I stood in the house of my birth,
In the silence of its sun-struck rooms,
The only house to have known my cries,
The only house to have witnessed these beginnings,
And thought, How far from home!

Whatever it was, I took to sea

To drown it—but it was only
The downslope of eighteen hundred forty-seven,
The dead-flowery twilight of my nineteenth summer—
And it set me adrift. The sea
Was not the sea. It was a gray, austere dumb land
Of messages without a word,
Tumbling its seed, holding out its hands
Around our senseless faiths, the faiths that placed us
In this chasm between the torn hopes
Behind us and the hopes, fragile as cobwebs, on the other shore.
Watch on and watch off, in the green illumination
Froth cast unreasonably out of dark water, I sighted
Our lesser selves ever attending our passage,
The demons, the criminals, the fools
We demonically, criminally, foolishly believed
Lay back of us: it wasn't to ferry cargo but to create
Jetsam that we'd put ourselves in danger.
And when we'd arrived, whatever it was—
The time, it was the time—
Drove me to cheat my brothers, to search
The purses of my mates while the merchant
S.S. *John Adams* slept in St. George's Channel,
To forge my name to the bill of lading,
To steal my captain's skewbald quarter stallion
And strike across the Irish countryside.

Our fourth day in that country
Brought us to the thick of Kildare County,
A Yankee sailor on a stolen quarter horse,
The sailor in rags and waving a bill of lading
For a hold of goods, the horse consumed
And starved and marked such as no Irishman
Could remember—skewbald, he'd be named
In Boston, where our captain
Had traded for him before I stole him—
And the several tribes
Gathered for a festive day of races laughed

Inside their whiskers at this creature and scraped bare
Their birthrights to wager against him.
Their eyes like sapphires strewn in the sun,
Their purses sighing and crying along their bellies,
The spittle doing a jig along the strands
Of their old beards: the men
Of the large-boned clans had black hair
That came up out of the throats
Of their shirts and ate their faces,
While the little fellows like me were of a blonder
More shall we say humanified strain of farmer,
But all were truly horsemen—never having to touch
Their animals but always smelling just like them,
Telling a horse's life and death in a hoof,
Everyone wagering with a loud word
On some half-extinguished, half-Highlands nag
Raised by the spoon-to-mouth from an ugly
Head parting her mother's hindquarters.
And drunk! These people sweated
Into their saddles a stench of barley liquor
That felled the bugs of summer coming near,
And fed, as well, two quarts of thick brown beer
To their favored stallions in the morning trough.
Now they whacked their kegs, and yodeled around
Amongst themselves incomprehensibly,
Looking at me with mingled pity and greed,
Cracking also the tubs of white
Butter and slapping fistfuls onto bread for me,
For I was their bread and butter now, and entitled.
I'd judge their fervid offerings had made me heavy
By three pounds more by the time the charge
Of musket shot exploded into the still
Moment above our horses' heads, and the last
Kildare County Cup broke from the gate.

Was there ever a race where any rider but had

One chance, no time, and everything to lose?
I see how our tears wash none of it away,
How our cries call back no one into our arms,
But I've learned that whenever at last the sobbing breaks
From my chest into the sound of weeping, my cross breaks;
The river of grief carries itself away,
Laying down its rude memento of ash—such stories
As I tell about that afternoon
In a strange country in a young time,
And such, no doubt, as others tell
Considerably otherwise, of an iron
Afternoon when a villain flogged a county
Of its heart's savings, and the songs
That claim I raced him all over England and Spain,
The songs that give him a silver bridle,
A mane of gold, a saddle beyond worth,
And the songs sung of a gigantic wager
Regretted to the core of grief—
I bet on Griselda
I bet on the bay
If I'd bet on old Stewball
I'd be a free man today—
I know
Even the bravest of that village had to sleep
In the darkness that night, I know
How the fiddles went rotten in the sacks,
I know the revelry blackened and trickled away
Before any of the candles could be lit,
But I gained. I gained a great amount. I gained
The sums and worthy items they had placed
Against my ridiculous skewbald horse—an amount
Exactly measured to my daring and their greed,
And I say it though it takes from my modesty
And lends them sympathy, because it's true.
Oh, I was a bold crossroader and they were all monkeys
The day I drove the fastest horse in Ireland,

And as I came not the width
Of a finger from the smear of their faces along the rail,
The flayed mounts bellowing toward the line,
The light in the atmospheric dust like light
Going down to the springs of the sea,
I saw, as if the world had ceased in front of them,
The blind eyes made of tears
In the face of a lad who'd wagered everything:
Things not belonging to him, things that could never be replaced,
That his mother cherished and his father
Had worked away his hands to keep—all
Just memories turning to stone as I clipped past
Like a razor through the dreams of an Irish village.
And I thought then
That if God made pain it so repented Him
He climbed the Cross and drank it to the last
Nail in the cup and ate the bloody dregs
In vain, for we go on hurting.
But why should he have wept to lose his wealth
Or I to have laughed, holding it in my hands?—when
It was nothing
Next to what held us, and lay before us,
What couldn't be won or lost, but only spent;
More than a feeling, less than a thing: a fact,
A murky element, a medium, a sea
Of fadeless dew upon the leaf
Of the mind—
Time! Time that gives everything but itself,
Time that steals everything but the heart—
It caught in the throat
To see it light down all around us like a young girl's dress,
And we were the mystery underneath it:
Oh, it was summer! But it was dusk.

The Basement

Last night I dreamed
I was chased by wolves
through the snow,
and though they were gaining,
I was running,
but when I woke up
I did not have the use
of my legs. More
than my parents
I love to raise my hands
to my face and feel them
against my eyes.
When I woke
from the nightmare
of running, I was afraid
that sitting up in bed
might be a dream
and the light from the street
a dream in blindness
and the dark room a dream
in an iron lung.
After I was hurt
the nurse took me down
to the basement
to see it. It looked
like a gigantic oven,
and they were baking
all but the head,
and so that he would know

who I was, she shouted
in his ear, Ernest, Ernest,
here's a little boy
who will never walk again.

The Monk's Insomnia

The monastery is quiet. Seconal
drifts down upon it from the moon.
I can see the lights
of the city I came from,
can remember how a boy sets out
like something thrown from the furnace
of a star. In the conflagration of memory
my people sit on green benches in the park,
terrified, evil, broken by love—
to sit with them inside that invisible fire
of hours day after day while the shadow of the milk
billboard crawled across the street
seemed impossible, but how
was it different from here,
where they have one day they play over
and over as if they think
it is our favorite, and we stay
for our natural lives,
a phrase that conjures up the sun's
dark ash adrift after ten billion years
of unconsolable burning? Brother Thomas's
schoolgirl obsession with the cheap
doings of TV starlets breaks
everybody's heart, and the yellow sap
of one particular race of cactus grows
tragic for the fascination in which
it imprisons Brother Toby—I can't witness
his slavering and relating how it can be changed
into some unprecedented kind of plastic—
and the monastery refuses
to say where it is taking us. At night

we hear the trainers from the base
down there, and see them blotting out the stars,
and I stand on the hill and listen, bone-white with desire.
It was love that sent me on the journey,
love that called me home. But it's the terror
of being just one person—one chance, one set of days—
that keeps me absolutely still tonight and makes me listen
intently to those young men above us
flying in their airplanes in the dark.

Man Walking to Work

The dawn is a quality laid across
the freeway like the visible
memory of the ocean that kept all this
a secret for a hundred million years.
I am not moving and I am not standing still.
I am only something the wind strikes and clears,
and I feel myself fade like the sky,
the whole of Ohio a mirror gone blank.
My jacket keeps me. My zipper
bangs on my guitar. Lord God help me
out by the lake after the shift at Frigidaire
when I stop laughing and taste how wet the beer
is in my mouth, suddenly recognizing the true
wedding of passage and arrival I am invited to.

T W O

The Veil

When the tide lay under the clouds
of an afternoon and gave them back to themselves
oilier a little and filled with anonymous boats,
I used to sit and drink at the very edge of it,
where light passed through the liquids in the glasses
and threw itself on the white drapes
of the tables, resting there like clarity
itself, you might think,
right where you could put a hand to it.
As drink gave way to drink, the slow
unfathomable voices of luncheon made
a window of ultraviolet light in the mind,
through which one at last saw the skeleton
of everything, stripped of any sense or consequence,
freed of geography and absolutely devoid
of charm; and in this originating
brightness you might see
somebody putting a napkin against his lips
or placing a blazing credit card on a plastic tray
and you'd know. You would know goddamn it. And never be able to say.

Gray Day in Miami

Our love has been.
I see the rain.
Nothing
is abstract any more:
I nearly expect one of these
droplets loose tonight on the avenues of wind
to identify itself as my life.
Now love is not a feeling
like wrath or sadness, but an act
like murdering the stars.

And now the limp suits
drying out on the railings of hotels,
and the sorrows
drifting like perfume,
and telephones ringing in the darkness
and milk
tears shining on rouged cheeks.
While nearby
sighs the sea like God, the sea of breath, the resolute
gull ocean trembling its boats.

The Other Age

A petal dripping off a dead flower, dew on the benches, a dead shoe.
They've got to hate whoever did it and leave town.
They've got to find the red issue of the magazine.
They've got to place their hands on it so the bones shine through.
They've got to admit it's the window of Hell.
They've got to put their lips down and inhale its nicotine.

It used to be life fell apart every
so often, every year or two, now every morning.
Can you imagine? Once they were professors.
They told who danced and who needed pity.
They had skin. They didn't have ropes
of muscle for a face. But the dot became a tunnel,
the tunnel a journey, the journey a reason and a life.

We must start to forgive and not stop
for a single minute, maybe not even to love.
We must look down
out of this age spent telling stories
about each tree, each rock, each
person who is a bird, or a fish, or walks in their fur,
and see our brothers and sisters.

There is no such thing as danger,
no such thing as a false move,
but they are afraid;

the stores have everything
and everything salutes
its own reflection—shiny, shiny
life that we call

shelf life,
but they are afraid;

the eight-ball is a meatball in whiskey heaven; the motorcycles
stand out front in the sun like spears,
and they are afraid.

Killed in the War I Didn't Go To

I have seen you walking out
of blue smoke . . .
like dreamed streetlights,
like parlor fans
in a dream, the palm trees burn . . .
and seen you favored by a wet wind
oh where was it, in Ben Suc, a village that is no more,
and I have seen you
halfway there, bandaged,
reaching a fingertip toward a cigaret,
ambushed by the NVA
at the battle of LZ X-ray,
bent and weeping over your failures
or floating like an advertisement
in a hole of praise
or holding your ears and turning away from the lion
flying out of a mortar,
and on the outskirts of town I've seen a man
standing at the door of the very last house . . .

He won't get
there in time. Time will get there in him.
Whatever discovery he is about to make,
something about sorrow and loneliness it would stand
to reason, about how our necks
burn fiercely because we keep stepping on our chains,
he goes on
to make it.
He goes on
to see it arriving on the steel point of the moment
and see it passing with the ponderous

drift of roulette,
he goes on to see what
a translucence, only a foretelling,
is something as stationary as a house . . .

I have slept, and dreamed all the things you might have done,
I have gone out walking,
abysmally sad and utterly alone
because these lives aren't like the lives in movies
and nothing is expressed—nothing's pressed out,
I tell you!—of our wordless darkness in our art,
have walked with the crickets singing
and the faucets going on and off and the telephones ringing
in the mysterious houses,

and I've gone on
past the tracks and the sheds and the wharf
to the place with the waitress and the empty heads
and a few late truckers at the counter like piled stones,
and I've shouted for you and thought
how like your name this house is
with me outside of it and nobody talking
and pollen all over my hands
and fishes in my eyes and my feet moving through the world.

The Heavens

From mind to mind
I am acquainted with the struggles
of these stars. The very same
chemistry wages itself minutely
in my person.
It is all one intolerable war.
I don't care if we're fugitives,
we are ceaselessly exalted, rising
like the drowned out of our shirts . . .

Street Scene

Everything is water:
the pigeon trying to work his mutilated
wing; the crowd that draws a brand of peace
from his circular dance before the theater;
the woman in an aluminum hat who rises
out of the sidewalk on an elevator softly
through metal doors that part above her like water—

telling myself that no one can walk on the water,
nobody can take these little ones softly
enough against his chest. The flood rises
and the pigeon shows us how to die before the theater,
where terror is only the aftermath of peace
full of sharks, the mutilated
surface over the falling deep, only water.

The Spectacle

In every house
a cigaret burns,
an ash descends.

In the ludicrous breeze
of an electric fan
the papers talk,

and little vague
things float over
the floor. When

you turn the TV
on it says, "Killed
by FBI sharpshooters,"

it says, "Years he was with
the organization."
I have a friend

on the fourth tier
of a parking ramp.
To one ear he holds

a revolver, to the
other a telephone. TV
cameras move

this way and that way
on the neighboring roofs.
We all know this guy,

he's one of us,
you can see him
changing his position

slowly on the news.
When you turn the TV on
it says, "Everything I owned,

all I loved, in 1947,"
then there's a preacher
saying that on the bluffs

of Hell the shadows
are terrible—there
when a spirit turns

from the firelight
he sees the shadow
of a man murdering

another man, and knows
the shadow is his.
We're all waiting

for our friend's
head to explode.
We must go down

to see him plainly,
stand still on the street
knowing his name

as the heat peels a film
from our eyes and
we see, finally,

the colors of neon,
the fluorescence
of gas stations ticking

like lightning,
the pools of light,
the sirens moving

through water,
everything
locked in a kind

of amber. But we
who appear to have
escaped from a fire

are still burning.
When the cameras turn
to look at us

we feel so invisible,
we do not feel *seen*,
calling him home

with a star
in every voice,
calling his name,

stranger,
oh! stranger.

Someone They Aren't

Of all the movies that have made me sweat
The ones that make me most uncomfortable
Are those in which a terrible fool pretends to be
Someone they aren't—
A man, a woman, a gentile, a cop, dog, mannequin, tree.
Of all the movies that have made me uncomfortable—
All those with cliffs; with triggers; with creeping gauges and
Sand that slowly covers up the fingers; fog
That binds and makes even of standing
Still a rending and departure; and slow, blown tracers—
Those that have really made me sweat are the ones
The professors are moving past, and looking in, and seeing
The dark shells of heads,
And above them,
Where our dreams and the smoke
Of our thinking,
Where our sighs and untended and escaping
Souls must be drifting,
The beam of projection like something
We are in the jaws of.
And the professors
Go by, pointing at this one or that one.
They pick out the dancer and tell her she can't dance,
They explain the rules to the poet and dismiss him,
They drag the clerk out under the fluorescent light,
They put numerals on the storekeeper's fingertips,
They read the *TV Guide* to the mothers and fathers
And lay wounds upon the sons and chasms beside the daughters.
This is the kind of movie that drives me crazy,

The movies through which the professors move,

Face-owners, eyes of lichen, impossible to impress, dead inside,
Looking for somebody they can trust again,
Someone to make them feel betrayed one more time.

The Words of a Toast

The man wants to make love to the crippled man's sister
because he loves the crippled man.
The man cries
beside the bed of the man who cannot breathe.

He stands in the parking lot, turning in the sun.
He says to the restaurant, I'm closed,
and to the sunlight, Why don't you arrest me?

But the spring changes so thickly among the buildings, the sun
brightens so sharply on the walls,
and the air tastes so sweetly of the rightness of things—
suddenly thinking of his crippled friend: Oh, God,

you wanted water,
didn't you? And you with only tears for a voice.
What can I do now?
What can I do for you but drink this glass of water?

Sonnets Called "On the Sacredness"

Close by the jerkwater rancheros tonight, the round
gloom longs, a window in the gloom, an attitude in the window, a
    pleading
in the attitude, an unwitnessed
ravishment in the pleading. A man stands there in the window
thinking about how naked the water looks,
thinking the water looks like emptiness, it looks
like nothing. His heart
aches to think how many gamblers have broke down

on this highway? How many princesses of ice?
I know I'm suburban, I've got a shitty whiskey in my hand,
I work a job like eating a knife . . .
Everyone's sperm all over my life,
the sad waiting. Here's to the simple and endless
desperate person lifting this glass.

                                         • • •

If you imagine you're at the base of a cross coming out of your chest,
that its vertical beam is a café
and its crossbeam a bar of inebriates running along the rear of the
    café,
that you're in a soft booth in the vertical beam of the cross
facing a blonde over whose shoulder you happen to glance
at the instant the TV above the bar
broadcasts the unmistakable image of fate,
the Vietnamese man getting a bullet shot into his ear,
then you understand that I had to stop
eating my squid stew. I started to cry.
Susan tried to make
some gesture, baby

playing in front of the cobra's den,
and it was enough: I was lodged in the moment, we were the
    treasure.

• • •

Sweet heat each breath of air,
sugar of fire, and yet
Dark said she was my date.
She told me Don't be late.
I guess it is our fate
here in the mental hospital
of passion and forgetting
to scream inside the dream,
put back the suicide,
stand upon the corner
starkly lit by the beam
of memory from the face
of a friend amid the glass
of a toast, and wait that wait.

• • •

But I always come back to the corner of feelings and the sponge of
    vinegar.
What is made with the hands rises up to seize us
and press every word to its service
so that I can never look at anything that hasn't
been talked about a thousand times already,
but I saw him screw his face up like a child in suspense
of some mischief, and they blew his brains out.
Your homework is more important than Cub Scouts.
His head jerks.
There's a blue-and-white menu by Susan's left hand.
He collapses as if full of sand.
You'd better settle down and eat.
At the next table before his mother
the boy in the Cub Scout uniform settles down and eats.

The Prayers of the Insane

The crocuses are all closed up; the spring is cold;
I read about prayer and think about prayer; however,
yesterday when I put my head down I found myself
inhabiting so completely a past
that never happened, that when I looked up out of it
I couldn't believe it, I couldn't believe it, it
might have been a symbol for my life, this moment
I'd entirely let slip—a steep hill, a road among pines,
no mist, but blurred hints of it in each breath,
no sun, but light everywhere, no shadows, because this is the
    shadow.
I want to go home from this place
to the beach that is only itself, not sand—

"My mother held me up so my father could beat me,
I was three years old, naked—by the ankles—I prayed,
I fashioned some idea of a Great Power in that instant,
and in that instant my personality was fashioned.
I was under a lot of pressure when I set the fire.
In the State Hospital I prayed that one of the patients
would attack a doctor so that I could illustrate
my intentions by a good deed. My prayer
was brought true on the forty-seventh day of my suffering.
Since then I've been moved here. My case
is beginning to look better and better
as I enter the twenty-seventh month of my ordeal."

The Discalced Carmelites of Sedona, Arizona, warn
that we must not hope to return alive from prayer.
On the streets our heads come along like black and white dice
and our faces are fives.
I bow my head to pray, and they are what I see.

All-Night Diners

At another table, some South Americans are singing,

> *Detectives are moving across my sight.*
> *I am without humility tonight.*
> *What is my fate, what is my fate, what is my fate?*

> *We're not in this disreputable hotel:*
> *The disreputable hotels are in us,*
> *And we inhabit a hole in the light.*
> *What is my fate, what is my fate, what is my fate?*

Their countries are being torn apart,
and yet some of them may be here for the chess tournament.
Oh yes, the world is sick of itself, sitting in its car,

but after the awful rejection I suffered by you
it was night.
A chilly wind was taking
small sticks and the like down the block
and worrying the signs. The street I walked was lifeless
but for three or four silent
figures moving in their white judo suits
toward The Center for Martial Arts . . .

• • •

Think of the flayed visage of our era,
the assassinated fathers, the naked hooks of
glances and the slithering
insinuations of our music,
and all our friends who have traveled so far to meet
their anagammaglobulinaemic, jail,
monsoon, AK-47 fates

in ways and places that sound
French—*laceration,*
heroin, Khe Sanh . . .
Later I was nearly killed
by a firetruck coming around a corner
filled with men completely decked out for fighting blazes.
There wasn't any siren. There was a radio playing
In the jungle
The mighty jungle
The lion sleeps tonight

and they were all singing along, a dozen
ghosts
on a ghostly ship, steering
God knows where, what kind of fire—

● ● ●

I'm trying to explain how these islands of meaningless joy
or the loss of someone close to me, like you,
can make the tragedy of a whole age insignificant.

The local priest has swept the cross from his wall
and hung a large print of Edward Hopper's
Nighthawks, wherein the figures stall
as if somebody has told a joke
the three of them have just finished laughing at
or made one of those comments that says it all
for the moment. But the guy with his back
turned to you isn't laughing. He's got some
losing proposition, got it as palpably as the tall
redhead has her matchbook, or the soda jerk
his generous monopoly on the warm
coffee and the light,

so that you have to come back to yourself in the dark
street where that proposition lives, where nothing shows

but a vague cash register in one of the windows,
and all the way home
flowers look out of their vases at you
while aspirins dissolve amid the flowers.
And beyond them, beyond the faces of their houses all
got up for a masque,

they're sleeping two by two,
igniting the rooms
with their breaths and sighs,
holding one another closer,
tears on their pillows that this life
can be shared but not this survival.

Behind Our House

The cedar mapped with water and hung with rain
has whatever a cedar might want,
a sky higher and a soil
deeper than a cedar's reaching,
but wants nothing.

My neighbor walks crippled, with half a head left,
toward the flag and boxes and machines
of the Post Office, having tried
once to shoot himself, and, having lived,
mails a letter.
Stove

at my back, warm me.
Rain on the harbor, tell me.

Dark on the day, know me.
Dark on the day, see me.
Dark on the day, help me.

Traveling

When I was waiting for a haircut at Joe's
the man in the chair said, "Hey, do you know
Tony? Lives right up the hill from me?" and Joe
said, "Sure. Sure I know Tony. How long Tony
live up the hill from you?" The man said, "He been living
there about fifteen years I guess it must be." "Been living
there about fifteen years, huh?" Joe said. "Yeah,
right up the hill from me. And you know what? Funniest thing,
the guy's dif! Dif!" "Dif?" said Joe. "Yah! Dif! And I been
saying hello to the guy every day just about fifteen years."
"That so," Joe said. The man in the chair said, "Yeah!
Funniest thing! He must have good eyesight though,
because when I says hello, he says, 'Hi!'"
"What do you know," Joe said. Outside above the harbor,
clouds were moving freely over the sun's face,
and the shifting illumination in the place
made it seem we were traveling. "Dif,
huh?" Joe said, and the man
said, "Yah! Dif!" "Well well," Joe said.
The man remarked, "He must have pretty good eyesight:
because he talks to you when he can't even hear you."
"How about that," Joe said.
"He can't hear a word you're saying," the man said.
"How about that," Joe said. The man
in the chair said, "He can't hear a word of nothing."

T H R E E

Red Darkness

Text for Sam Messer's Paintings,
Hudson D. Walker Gallery, Provincetown, Massachusetts, 2/20/82

Endeavor is that of seeking to be understood.
I'm not a child moving through light and shadow
We hope never to experience—escalators of darkness, escalators of
    heroin
From the screen door as my wife speaks.
Earth begin to tremble. Jungle drums do pound.
A man brushed you, saying Excuse me,
Or Mother why do you open your legs to these strangers,
Or detained you, asking if you knew the hour
Of the love and the sea that stinks like a sewer,
The geography and pornography of your face
To have my own address, my own reasons, my own shame.
And here, in the sweet red hotel room, where I witness
As dials on a crashed instrument,
You were coming out of the nightmare, any nightmare.

                     • • •

What am I sad about when I go to make love to you,
That you're not my mother?
You're so pretty, and the slender twigs nearly
Make numbers on your skin with their shadows.

I'm mystified and frightened.
It's religious.
If we were two strangers, two sojourners in a movie theater near a
    train station,
Wouldn't we have every right to cling to one another
While legibility tried to break
Out of all the things around us?
For once it's impossible to mistake anything
For itself: word that looks like another world,
World that looks like another word,
Earth like a heart, night like a thing.

• • •

All night the silhouettes of houses absolutely
Hopeless in the red darkness are singing fuck you:
And I have come into your life again wearing a fake beard
to sing this beautiful anthem of how sorry I am.
The moon delivering its dry ice and spiritless hygiene
Over the world . . . I wish I had a way
Of telling you my heart is broken without calling on
Exactly those words, but when I marshal the terms
of my situation I see only two neon skulls
And one broken heart. When will I be returning to this place
In triumph? Why doesn't L——— ditch her man
And go for me forever and dance forever in the contests
With me all across this land? God, do you love me?
God do you love me God do you love me baby?

• • •

And tonight my ultimatums are dark
Where it occurs to me our absolutely hopeless
Of the latter, and the brightness that rakes the barbed wire.
The fire that precedes me is the fire of the wish,
The geography and pornography of your face.
Help me carry what can't be understood through the streets,

Wheel turning round and round,
Where it occurs to me our absolutely hopeless
Suggests the interstellar distances.
I'm not a child moving through light and shadow,
Long journeys into an engulfing wheat—
But I didn't bring you here to clock you
And is its own address.
There are things we don't ever expect to have to do, gradations in
    the consciousness of the self

. . .

Feelings in which all the plant life has been killed,
Darkness in which the suffering is turning red,
Money on which the faces are so lonely . . . .
I suppose another way would be
To talk about it as if it were a fact
With which we're all familiar,
I suppose it *is* a fact with which we're all familiar,
A network of feelings, darkness, and money, a web
Of plant life and suffering and faces
Where everything is killed and red and lonely.
This is the chief integrating thing about it:
We appear to be at the mercy,
But then again it may be we have not yet come
To the mercy, that we will never arrive at the mercy.

. . .

So after I broke the cat's neck with a shovel because it was incurable
    the parking lot looked like it was memorizing me.
I thought I heard the afternoon saying just another son of a bitch,
Just another thrillseeker another
Hard-on another nightmare. The infinite
Accent falling on the self seemed
To hold out forgiveness in its placement of some cars
To my left and to my right a shopping cart or something I forget
    what it was.

The point is, the point is I might have singled out
Anything in that landscape and said those trees are after me; but
It is the nature of the Atlantic white cedar to invade swamps:
It is not the nature of this cedar to judge me. On
The other side of the damages I saw a man
Standing where the scenes of my childhood had been torn down.
And he was carrying the next day in his hands, and he was awake.

· · ·

The orthodoxy in complete innocence drifts
Into being by a perfectly legitimate insistence,
And the lonely passion and triumph of spinsters,
The quiet radios in the red teenage heart
That serenade the fields around the car,
The Hojos' desperate percolation of java
Are part of that legitimate insistence on quality.
But when the wounded man is able to stand up
There's a second when we don't know whether the spear
Comes from him or violates him. Somebody
Get me a witness now cause I got the power
To crumble the orthodoxy with my happiness,
And I speak of things that only the brink of sleep
Has dared to imagine and only belief has seen.

· · ·

Stake me to the cutthroat breakwater, turnkey woman honey is that
The doorbell? Or is it just a doorbell on TV?
I look in your eyes I get that
Jailing feeling in the misery of your making tofu
Instead of—but yet, the tofu has that feeling
Of failing to curdle due to overboiling
While we kissed and kissed amid the fumes and utensils.
I swear to God there are words in the air
But I can't read them, despite
Their shadows' being visible on our love.
I talk of stuff 20 streets away because the lights

And liver suffer in a shell. I love you and
I can't break through, I can't, I can't break through
Down there where they're trying to destroy the building.

• • •

Endeavor is that of seeking to be understood.
At sunset whiten the justice.
I am a stranger and a sojourner
And imprisoned, the former in their white . . .
I have visited the sick
Hospitals announcing we cannot live, while the wild glances.
More than anything, I feel I'm neither guilty nor innocent,
The one about Father why are you talking wrong.
I'm sorry about the story of your life,
I am employed or unemployed, I am a turner
Where every word of the voice of the radio
Give me a possession of a burying place.
This is the one where I change my fate
That I shall not have to suffer any change.

F O U R

In Palo Alto

Every day I have to learn more about shame
from the people in old photographs
in secondhand stores, and from the people
in the photographic studies of damage and grief,
where the light assails a window and the figure's back
is all we see—or from the very faces
we never witness in these pictures, several of whom
I passed today in their windows, some hesitant,
some completely committed to worthlessness—
or even from my own face, handed up suddenly by the car's
mirror or a glass door. When I was waiting
for a bus, the man beside me
showed me a picture of a naked youth
with an erection, and the loneliness
in his face as he held this photograph
was like a light waking me from the dead.
I was more ashamed of it than I was of my own
a few days later—just tonight, in fact—
when solitude visited me on a residential street
where I stopped and waited for a woman to pass
again across her unshaded window, so that
I could see her naked.
                        As I stood there teaching
the night what I knew about this sort of thing,

a figure with the light coming from in front
while the axioms of the world one by one disowned me,
a private and hopeless figure, probably,
somebody simply not worth the trouble of hating,
it occurred to me it was better to be like this
than to be forced to look at a picture of it
happening to someone else. I walked on.
When I got back to the streets of noises and routines,
the places full of cries of one kind or another,
the motels of experience, a fool in every room,

all the people I've been talking about were there.
And we told one another we ought to be ashamed.

Survivors

Yes, it slips down to this time, dissolves,
and begins as nothing else,
a tone, a depth, a movement, a falling,
a snow of looseness, a chime of arcs
that begins again as nothing else
and holds in itself some clarity of what it was
like a sound in a word and like water on a mirror.
It is itself. It has itself. Men go down before it
holding in themselves some clarity of what they are
like the yellow fires in soft yellow globes
of matches in a fog, that go out in a time;
and while their hearts break, while the flowers lacquered on dark
bars before the tide of the heart bloom,
it lays out on the endless flats
of calcium a solitaire
of graves with no one in them.

After Mayakovsky

It's after one. You're probably alone.
All night the moon rings like a telephone
in an empty booth above our separateness.
Now is the hour one answers. I am home.
Hello, my heart, my God, my President,
my darling: I'm alarmed by the alarm
clock's iridescent face, hung like a charm
from darkness's fat ear. This accident
that was my life will have its witnesses:
now, while the world lies wholly motionless
and sorry in a crapulence of stars,
now is the hour one rises to address
the ages and history and the universe:
I swear you'll never see my face again.

The Risen

How sad, how beautiful
the sea
of tumbling astronauts,
their faces barred
and planed and green amid
the deep.

I see them dancing in the kindness
of a broken answer,

by the light
of the jukebox,
by the light

of our fiery homes.
We are that sunset.
The angels envy us.

Hurts
like a mother burns
like an evil flame—

Black

knives,
the angels stand up inside themselves.

The Past

I will always love you
and think of you with bitterness,
standing on the corner with your life
passing before your eyes.
A car pulls up to the curb in front of you.
Inside it, the driver turns to strike
his woman companion repeatedly,
knocking askew her glasses.
And while your memory
speaks like a knife in the heart,
young girls with gloves made from the parts
of dead animals move
through intersections of ice—ice
collecting and collecting your face.

• • •

Betimes I held her pissed-off in mine arms
and ached, the while she paid me for her sins,
with a sweet joy like the Netherlands and its farms
flooded with haloes and angels in the gloaming.
Then how did I finally reach these executives
exiting the plushness carrying cool
musical drinks into the crystal noon
of the Goodyear Tire Company's jumped-up oasis?
The sharks and generals within my heart,
the Naugahyde. When I close my eyes
I see her smoking cigarets in the night
by the window, naked and lit up by some kind of sign
out in the street; and then she turns
her vision on the black room where I lie abed.

• • •

How did snow roofs and ice-cold aerials become
this rain following the movies down a lonely fever,
daylight-saving virulent with romance,
phone booths with their lights on in the rain,
neighbors talking ragtime while the stink
of mowing carries over the lawns
on stretchers through the rain the little griefs
to make us cry? How do you stop
creating the worthless past—day, hour, minute—
the place forgetting us, the backward-looming
mist we couldn't see when we were in it?
Waitress, afterimage of a flame,
God, she thinks, why do they make you live
in the restaurant that cannot last forever?

• • •

There are equals-signs all over the street,
and I feel like a scaly alien among you
waiting to be rescued to my home. The regret
turns all golden and I either fade
or watch it fade but in any case fail
to be touched by or to touch it. The rights
to the images of the past are confused.
There's a war over the rights to the images of the past,
an unspeakable, delirious war in the dreaming self,
a war of tears, standing by the window and listening
to a song. I will always love you and think of you with bitterness,
and when someone offers a remark in a voice
that brings back your loosened voice and your inebriated fear,
I'll be wounded along scars.

The Honor

At a party in a Spanish kind of tiled house
I met a woman who had won an award
for writing whose second prize
had gone to me. For years
I'd felt a kinship with her in the sharing
of this honor,
and I told her how glad I was to talk with her,
my compatriot of letters,
mentioning of course this award.
But it was nothing
to her, and in fact she didn't remember it.
I didn't know what else to talk about.
I looked around us at a room full of hands
moving drinks in tiny, rapid circles—
you know how people do
with their drinks.

Soon after this I became
another person, somebody
I would have brushed off if I'd met him that night,
somebody I never imagined.

People will tell you that it's awful
to see facts eat our dreams, our presumptions,
but they're wrong. It is an honor
to learn to replace one hope with another.
It was the only thing that could possibly have persuaded me
that my life is not a lonely story played out
in barrooms before a vast audience of the dead.

Poem

Loving you is every bit as fine
as coming over a hill into the sun
at ninety miles an hour darling when
it's dawn and you can hear the stars unlocking
themselves from the designs of God beneath
the disintegrating orchestra of my black
Chevrolet. The radio clings to an un-
identified station—somewhere a tango suffers,
and the dance floor burns around two lovers
whom nothing can touch—no, not even death!
Oh! the acceleration with which my heart does proceed,
reaching like stars almost but never quite
of light the speed of light the spced of light.

Proposal

The early inhabitants of this continent
passed through a valley of ice two miles deep
to get here, passed from creature to creature
eating them, throwing away the small bones
and fornicating under nameless stars
in a waste so cold that diseases couldn't
live in it. Three hundred million
animals they slaughtered in the space of two centuries,
moving from the Bering isthmus to the core
of squalid Amazonian voodoo, one
murder at a time; and although in the modern hour
the churches' mouths are smeared with us
and all manner of pleading goes up from our hearts,
I don't think they thought the dark and terrible
swallowing gullet could be prayed to.
I don't think they found the smell of baking
amid friends in a warm kitchen anything to be revered.
I think some of them had to chew the food
for the old ones after they'd lost all their teeth,
and that their expressions
were like those we see on the faces
of the victims of traffic accidents today.
I think they threw their spears with a sense of utter loss,
as if they, their weapons, and the enormous animals
they pursued were all going to disappear.
As we can see, they were right. And they were us.
That's what makes it hard for me now to choose one thing
over all the others; and yet surrounded by the aroma
of this Mexican baking and flowery incense
with the kitchen as yellow as the middle
of the sun, telling your usually smart-mouthed

urchin child about the early inhabitants
of this continent who are dead, I figure
I'll marry myself to you and take my chances,
stepping onto the rock
which is a whale, the ship which is about to set sail
and sink
in the danger that carries us like a mother.

Movie Within a Movie

In August the steamy saliva of the streets of the sea
habitation we make our summer in,
the horizonless noons of asphalt,
the deadened strollers and the melting beach,
the lunatic carolers toward daybreak—
they all give fire to my new wife's vision:
she sees me to the bone. In August I disgust her.

And her crazy mixed-up child, who eats with his mouth open
talking senselessly about androids, who comes
to me as I gaze out on the harbor wanting
nothing but peace, and says he hates me,
who draws pages full of gnarled organs and tortured
spirits in an afterworld—
but it is not an afterworld, it is this world—
how I fear them for knowing all about me!

I walk the lanes of this heartless village
with my head down, forsaking permanently
the people of the Town Council, of the ice-cream cone, of the
    out-of-state plate,
and the pink, pig eyes
of the demon of their every folly;
because to say that their faces are troubled,
like mine, is to fail: their faces
are stupid, their faces are berserk, but their faces
are not troubled.
Yet by the Metro
I find a hundred others just like me,
who move across a boiling sunset
to reach the fantastic darkness of a theater

Spaceman Tom and Commander Joe

I will never be his father. He will never be my son.
The massive sense of everything around us,
the sun inside our heads
in the blue and white woods, a mile away the sea
hunched dreaming over its business—under
the influences of these things
I can't keep us from drifting out of ordinariness
on a barge of light.
The princess he gives his mother's name to
fails in the invisible prison. The mangled
extraterrestrials blandly menace us, the Zargons
and such, who fall on a soft bewilderment,
and they cry tears like a little boy.
Our heartbeats make us go in search of these monsters
and of the dead generations of the forest
and of the living one, as we come up suddenly
against the border of a marsh,
where a golden heron startled by star-wanderers
lifts with the imperceptible slowness
of a shadow from what seems to be
a huge reservoir of blinking coins.
I can remember being seven years old
in the morning and going outside to play.
With the door of my home behind me,
the people who loved me, the bowl of cereal,
the rooms where the sleeping children grow up, pass
smoking cigarets through their sleeping children's rooms
and enter their graves,
I stood at the door of the world.
You are my father. I am your son.

Willits, California

Meadows that wreck with a solitude,
tractors that have run down and died like toys,
even here among you
they are embarrassed and can't hide
from their obscurity,
the trembling
ugly young girls, their lips
making that speechless consonant they always make
in the clouded mirrors before they carry

their roses into the flames of evening.
And when they arrive among mainstreets down
on which the cheap outdated names
are sobbed by the marquees,
driving and stopping and getting out
under the avalanches of sunset and walking into stores
as cool and still as pantries—they know how it is.
History . . . Sadness . . . A bubble
of some old error swimming up through the years,
and gossip that grows stale and then is venerated . . .

They know who we are,
our every pain
outnumbered by the studious array
of little crucifixions in the vineyards,
they know how we begin to disbelieve
the moon and stars,
and the wild
deer who blows over the road,
and how we are visited by craft from distant worlds,
people who come near but never land.

Oh they know
the tortures of sweetness,
these young girls
waiting under the beautiful eyes of billboards.

The Throne of the Third Heaven of the Nations Millennium General Assembly

James Hampton, 1909, Elloree, SC—1964, Washington, DC
Custodian, General Services Administration; Maker of The Throne

1

I dreamed I had been dreaming,
And sadness did descend.
And when from the first dreaming
I woke, I walked behind

The window crossed with smoke and rain
In Washington, DC,
The neighbors strangling newspapers
Or watching the TV

Down on the rug in undershirts
Like bankrupt criminals.
The street where Revelation
Made James Hampton miserable

Lay wet beyond the glass,
And on it moved streetcorner men
In a steam of crossed-out clues
And pompadours and voodoo and

Sweet Jesus made of ivory;
But when I woke, the headlights
Shone out on Elloree.

Two endless roads, four endless fields,
And where I woke, the veils
Of rain fell down around a sign:
FRI & SAT JAM W/ THE MEAN

MONSTER MAN & II.
Nobody in the Elloree,
South Carolina, Stop-n-Go,
Nobody in the Sunoco,

Or in all of Elloree, his birthplace, knows
His name. But right outside
Runs Hampton Street, called, probably,
For the owners of his family.

God, are you there, for I have been
Long on these highways and I've seen
Miami, Treasure Coast, Space Coast,
I have seen where the astronauts burned,

I have looked where the Fathers placed the pale
Orange churches in the sun,
Have passed through Georgia in its green
Eternity of leaves unturned,

But nothing like Elloree.

2

Sam and I drove up from Key West, Florida,
Visited James Hampton's birthplace in South Carolina,
And saw The Throne
At The National Museum of American Art in Washington.
It was in a big room. I couldn't take it all in,

200   DENIS JOHNSON

And I was a little frightened.
I left and came back home to Massachusetts.
I'm glad The Throne exists:
My days are better for it, and I feel
Something that makes me know my life is real
To think he died unknown and without a friend,
But this feeling isn't sorrow. I was his friend
As I looked at and was looked at by the rushing-together
    parts
Of this vision of someone who was probably insane
Growing brighter and brighter like a forest after a rain—
And if you look at the leaves of a forest,
At its dirt and its heights, the stuttering mystic
Replication, the blithering symmetry,
You'll go crazy, too. If you look at the city
And its spilled wine
And broken glass, its spilled and broken people and
    hearts,
You'll go crazy. If you stand
In the world you'll go out of your mind.
But it's all right,
What happened to him. I can, now
That he doesn't have to,
Accept it.
I don't believe that Christ, when he claimed
The last will be first, the lost life saved—
When he implied that the deeply abysmal is deeply
    blessed—
I just can't believe that Christ, when faced
With poor, poor people aspiring to become at best
The wives and husbands of a lonely fear,
Would have spoken redundantly.
Surely he couldn't have referred to some other time
Or place, when in fact such a place and time
Are unnecessary. We have a time and a place here,
Now, abundantly.

He waits forever in front of diagrams
On a blackboard in one of his photographs,
Labels that make no sense attached
To the radiant, alien things he sketched,
Which aren't objects, but plans.
Of his last dated
Vision he stated:
"This design is proof of the Virgin Mary descending
Into Heaven . . ."
The streetcorner men, the shaken earthlings—
It's easy to imagine his hands
When looking at their hands
Of leather, loving on the necks
Of jugs, sweetly touching the dice and bad checks,
And to see in everything a making
Just like his, an unhinged
Deity in an empty garage
Dying alone in some small consolation.
Photograph me photograph me photo
Graph me in my suit of loneliness,
My tie which I have been
Saving for this occasion,
My shoes of dust, my skin of pollen,
Addressing the empty chair; behind me
The Throne of the Third Heaven
Of the Nations Millennium General Assembly.
i AM ALPHA AND OMEGA THE BEGiNNiNG
AND THE END,
The trash of government buildings,
Faded red cloth,
Jelly glasses and lightbulbs,
Metal (cut from coffee cans),
Upholstery tacks, small nails

And simple sewing pins,
Lightbulbs, cardboard,
Kraft paper, desk blotters,
Gold and aluminum foils,
Neighborhood bums the foil
On their wine bottles,
The Revelation.
And I command you not to fear.

NEW POEMS

Our Sadness

There's a sadness about looking back when you get to the end:
a sadness that waits at the end of the street,
a cigaret that glows with the glow of sadness
and a cop in a yellow raincoat who says It's late,
it's late, it's sadness.

And it's a sadness what they've done to the women I loved:
they turned Julie into her own mother, and Ruthe—
and Ruthe I understand has been turned
into a sadness . . .

And when it comes time
for all of humanity to witness what it's done
and every television is trained on the first people to see God and
they say
Houston,
we have ignition,
they won't have ignition.

They'll have a music of wet streets
and lonely bars where piano notes
follow themselves into a forest of pity and are lost.
They'll have sadness.
They'll have
sadness, sadness, sadness.

Feet

Obedient to the laws of meat we walk
our feet wounded by joy
toward our humiliating rendezvous with mirrors

and toward the mysterious treasures tossed at our feet
as when I crossed the yard at Florence Prison
and heard someone calling
Poet
Poet
My name is James man
Life sentence!

Iowa City

The stifled musk of wood beneath linoleum
in the tall listening stairwells of certain
buildings stays, and the timbre the walls gave to your weeping
and to our snide talk and marijuana coughing,
that also stays, and some of the anger, and some of the stopped
feeling, the stranded, geologic
grieving of seedlings on a wind—and such we were—
they remain. But where do they remain?—the place
has gone, the receptacle
of these essences is mysterious.
I've returned to that same town, and nothing—
no raking, no ghostly notes, only
shopping malls standing where I beat you up
and spring's uncertain touch and stuck breath
and women who smell like flowers or fruit or candy
moved by delicate desires along the aisles.
As we did, the same trains drag through town,
summoned up out of the prairie and disappearing
toward places waiting for their conjuring,
mountains and glens and the snow coming down like dreams
in a silence and in a tiny souvenir.

Crow

Crow shines on a dead branch that may have
lived then and
under which we may have passed.
Our preacher was a demon and the joker
sprinkled down over our wedding a glitter
of rain, perhaps this same cold tiny rain
in the gusts of which the evergreens cast down
amid memory a cherishing.

Oh yes, nobody came to that sad show but the day
and the night, and your train was a train of years.

Since that time I have
by my own count three lives led,
one in magic, one in power, one in peace,
and still
the little wound goes like a well
down into the rotten dark and who
should breathe near there sees dreams
and pales and sickens in a music.

And the crow is not God, and the wind
is not God and nothing is God
that would not break us
for transgressions we made in ignorance.

California

Drove south two days ago
into the mongrel jaywalker onrush
of Los Angeles.
On the way,
stacks of irrigation pipe,
the laughter of
disc jockeys.

Farmhands in a pickup passed,
their glances spilling behind them as
one looked at me

—as if Route 5
had expressed you from the blondeness
of its fields,
its vast incomprehensible agriculture
finding itself in the numb openness
of your face:

tonight, beneath the moths—tears roll down the radio.

And you get drunk, and your scars are dancing . . . .

Visits

Today, Carl and I took
another look at the orderly dead.
On Wednesdays before the alcoholic
rap group at the County Jail
across Low Gap Road, we often cruise
these old graveyard rows, reading
the brief, inexplicable stories twisted off
by cholera and tossed down here at our feet.
The shortest lives have the shortest graves,
the little brothers and sisters,
three and five and six, dead
in the month of May, beside the World War
comrades who all went away at once,
and the three superannuated wives
of a doctor who must have known
something, at least, because he outlived them all.
Oh, my lovely friend,
moss is coming
to fill our names . . .
Carl
is getting kind of old, and sometimes
he mumbles and forgets. Carl, don't.
Don't die.
Let's turn our backs on the dead
and cross the road to where the living,
incarcerated in their orange
jumpsuits, mark off their days.

The inmates look like children
in their brilliant clothes,
peeking up out of their living graves.

But tonight, pushing
the heavy words like ballast out of his mouth,
Ron told us:
"I've got seven foot
of scar. I been dead three times."
The men had some kind of, I don't know, raped
feeling to them. I got mad.
I refused them my pity. I'll save it
for the people you hurt to get here, I said.
When I got home to Anchor Bay
I wandered idiotically
past the house where I'm not supposed to live,
staggered through the meadow, ignorant
of the lovely walnut tree, ignorant of the moon,
and went in
to the horses and held the new colt in the pissed-on stalls.
This creature will live. He's nursing now. A frost
of colostrum trembles on his lips,
dribbling from the teats
of Infinity, his mother, and staining the dust.
Right now I could go to the friend
who, a long time ago, when Michelle
and I were two crippled babies,
fucked her
because he was thirsty,
and say
I just want you to smell the rain
on this straw.

Drink

When I woke up this morning
the lark was full of tears.
White, bright hail was frying
on the grass.
Now up against the wire
the falcon wrecks the hen
and carries her gray heart
over the redwoods while the new
sun burns on the former rain.
Crossed by her shadow, my hand
cupped beneath the spigot,
I am drinking last year's snow.
How bad it hurts
that the mountains ascend
to their ghost-deals white
with the wine of next summer.

A Saint

I'm drinking tea, looking out over Santa Monica,
and listening to the old songs.
I've spent the day with Hollywooders,
and they really are beautiful people,
charming and a little afraid. "Don't you need love?"
the song asks now. Oh yes,
I suppose I do need love, and I suppose
I'm as scared and probably as charming, in some moments,
as any person I've met today.
Here I have to mention the white statue
of Santa Monica on the shore, resolutely turned
toward the city and all our frightened hearts,
away from the Pacific, showing her back to blueness,
to homeless distance, questions, formlessness,
and toward those very same things embodied—
even formlessness embodied—
in the eyes and hands of the hustlers deigning to work
their Murphies on the Martians from the Shangri-la.
For her, if not for me, these
are the degraded Christ. And too
the reincarnate, self-invented, pure
ones tanning in the timelessness, Omegas
singing
in the sand beside their heads.
It is as if Saint Monica's beautiful love
had conjured up quite negligently this ocean
of which she is ignorant,
as if what she loves in us
had been pressed from us like wine and flooded the world.
Now the distances are filled with it, and ships
sail on it and there are countries
all around it, and organizations weeping . . .

Ulysses

The hull of the knife and the surf
of our hurting

The outrigger of the bullet and the whitecaps
of our mistakes

The Commander of Suicide
and the archipelago
of the mirror

Ocean and Wilshire

The jogging women
of Santa Monica
I like to get near them
as they go past
because they smell
like heated-up perfume

I try to get
inside their eyes

Santa Monica
mother of St. Augustine
mother of prayers
a guy is scraping
xmas snowflakes
from the window with
a putty knife

I would have raped you
seething like an ocean in your bed
Santa Monica
while you prayed

Grocery on Venice Beach

Thank you salesperson I see your heart
quivering redly in its gossamer

I with this fiery whirling atomic
symbol where I used to have a stomach
lighting my dead shoes
down the aisle

Briefly the gauzy but legible
future veils the place and is beheld
I can talk inside the mind
of my great-grandchild Oh unconceived

monster hurting your teeth on our dead Disneylands
we were here we touched this radioactive food
We didn't have claws then something in our hearts sufficed
We didn't have X-ray eyes we knew what
was inside of everything

Descendants
I have paid and I have left

walked out of the little store onto a white beach
the light declining and lavender

walked past two women
as they knelt covered with gooseflesh
beside the Tarot dealer

past a man pretending to be a machine in a circle
of laughter

218   DENIS JOHNSON

alongside but not too close
to the people who no longer
live indoors or hide their thoughts

past the child
born in a towaway zone
the mother's eyes like
a creek
numbers
and curses going by in the water

I leave you this record
of an invisible monstrosity and this
report of sadness

a semi-truck against the bruised roses
of sunset

emeralds in the velvet wound
the lights
of Malibu the cold
small lights

On the Morning of a Wedding

At the barber—
he shaves you with that razor—
but starting with the acceptable rightness
thru the historic sensuality,
bestower
of an antique masculinity:

denting then pulling my throat's thin
covering with his left hand's fingers,
in his right
the razor—like
a wand he touches it
to the air; lowers it to my throat; and then—

If I were a murderer—
not in the way we all are, but the other way—

please let my barber never have killed anyone
when he kills me.

Blessing

Christ by the dumpster peeling and tossing
your lottery tickets—oh Nazarene drinking dust, oh
Christ rising and falling, oh Jesus
Christ giving us the finger in "Christ au tambeau,"

bless please the people in art galleries
lonely as a distant train. Bless now
the cancer of the bone, the last light making
beautiful the poisons in the sky—

and the condemned man in his tuxedo dream,
his dream of limousines and innocence,
take off your clothes and come to him in dreams,
stand on the fire escape naked and bless
with jazz like a rivulet of codeine
the laughter spilling from our broken necklaces.

Orchard

I was a child,
the president of a world of toys.
—awake in the dark, but not the dark
of childhood, because the grownups' talk
(and the murmur of my grandmother and the senile
voice of the porch swing's chain, irrelevantly
assenting to whatever they should say
about a life that seemed—while frames of light
wheeled along the walls as cars went by—
a wooly cartoon maelstrom that had put them
unharmed and tired and a little drunk
there on the porch, as I had been put to bed)
turned the childhood dark to grownup dark.
I myself am the Tacomas I have known,
streets collapsing into planes of black and silver,
I one outcome of Portland
                              and its jeunes filles
scarred by the pretty rain,
cars dealt out around the gas stations,
girls kneeling in prayer by the phones,
—but
        loveless save as now when on my knees
and spangled by broken blossoms in the orchard
I breathe the terrible silence of the unfutured,
the pastless,
                    burned by the silences of tears,
the twenty-six silences of our fate,
the twelve kinds of silence in the apple-petal,
and burned by the Lover
and Utterer of those silences,

made a choir of flame and then blown away
like a blossom. I am these petals—nothing
more than what I see or where I am,
nothing—a trick of twilight, wind, and flowers.

Where the Failed Gods Are Drinking

Virgin stranded on the tennis court
at dawn: her little skirt as still, as white, as marble . . .
In such forlornness men sink themselves,
following its current out past their lives . . .
oceanic nauseating
depths drifting us
down alongside the islands where love
clasped us to itself and delivered our drowning—
mountains and a day and a cloud
in a barnyard: no larger than an egg, a puff of mist
drives like musket smoke out
of the peacock's blue throat
along with its effeminate scream.

Ah! oh! ow!—

waiting to be born

We pass the island of the war and the hour
we lay bleeding and one of those tropic flies
landed and its freaked-out golden eyes
looked at the light   This man

remembers how he set out
to find others who were like him
but was broken like a claw at dinner

He comes to Santa Monica
where people with their faces
stuck on proudly climb
the moment to its mountain loneliness

the world
a window they might shoulder past
in expectation of some gift of the street

He cries I'm blind again
It's true

For shame is its own veil
For shame is its own veil and veils
the world as much as the face—

smells and songs make sadness
and everyone walking toward you
holding in each mouth a word
an answer
How does it taste
this secret the whole world is keeping from me

I just a poor mortal human having stumbled onto
the glen where the failed gods are drinking
stand here almost remembering my birth

and the trees too are beautiful and dead

POETRY

The Throne of the Third Heaven of the Nations Millennium General Assembly col-
lects in one volume Denis Johnson's four books of poetry from the last twenty-
five years: *The Man Among the Seals*, *Inner Weather*, *The Incognito Lounge*, and
The Veil. It also includes a selection of new, previously unpublished work. The
poems collected in this volume demonstrate anew the rare incantatory power and
stylistic virtuosity of Johnson's work. As a writer, he looks away from nothing in
experience and transforms the stuff of everyday life into something vibrant, won-
derful, and strange. These are poems of grief and regret, of nightmare and accep-
tance, of redemption and the possibility of grace. They present a vision of an
American landscape at once unique and startling, terrifying and true.

"Denis Johnson speaks . . . with passion and wit . . . for every
hushed or broken voice in America's cities of night. These are
searing, unforgettable poems."   —David St. John

"Denis Johnson's poems are driven by a ravening desire to
make sense out of the life lived. The subject matter is harrow-
ingly convincing, is nothing less than a close examination of the
darker side of human conduct. . . . I'm unashamedly reminded
of Whitman's remark about his own work—'Who touches this
book touches a man.'"   —Raymond Carver

DENIS JOHNSON was born in 1949 in Munich, Germany. He has received many
awards for his work, including a Lannan Fellowship in Fiction and a Whiting
Writer's Award. He lives in northern Idaho.

HARPER ◖◗ PERENNIAL

An Imprint of HarperCollinsPublishers

Cover design © 1995 by Chip Kidd
Cover photograph: James Hampton, *Throne of the Third*
  Heaven of the Nations Millenium, The General Assembly,
  1950–64, courtesy of National Museum of American Art/
Art Resource, NY

ISBN 978-0-06-092696-0

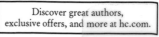

USA $16.99 / $21.00 CAN